Narrative Transvestism

*Rhetoric and Gender
in the Eighteenth-Century
English Novel*

Madeleine Kahn

Cornell University Press

ITHACA AND LONDON

First published 1991 by Cornell University Press.

International Standard Book Number 0-8014-2536-0 (cloth)
International Standard Book Number 0-8014-9770-1 (paper)
Library of Congress Catalog Card Number 91-55060

Printed in the United States of America

Librarians: Library of Congress cataloging information appears on the last page of the book.

♾ The paper in this book meets the minimum requirements of the American National Standard for Information Sciences—Permanence of Paper for Printed Library Materials, ANSI Z39.48.1984.

Library of Congress Cataloging-in-Publication Data

Kahn, Madeleine, 1955–
    Narrative transvestism : rhetoric and gender in the eighteenth-century English novel / Madeleine Kahn.
        p.   cm. — (Reading women writing)
    Includes bibliographical references and index.
    ISBN 0-8014-2536-0 (alk. paper). — ISBN 0-8014-9770-1 (pbk. : alk. paper)
        1. English fiction—18th century—History and criticism.   2. Women and literature—Great Britain—History—18th century.   3. English fiction—Men authors—History and criticism.   4. Richardson, Samuel, 1689–1761. Clarissa.   5. Defoe, Daniel, 1661?–1731. Roxana.   6. First person narrative.   7. Sex role in literature.   8. Narration (Rhetoric)   9. Women in literature.   I. Title.   II. Series.
    PR858.W6K34   1991
    823'.509—dc20   91–55060

For my sisters, who keep the giggle quotient high.

Contents

Acknowledgments

Two people in particular helped me over the intellectual and emotional hurdles I had to leap to complete this project. For letting me borrow from their stores of wisdom and of faith in me, my deepest gratitude goes to Marilynne Kanter and Trudy Palmer.

I also owe thanks to many others who were generous with their work and with themselves, and who laughed at my jokes: Elizabeth Heckendorn Cook and Jon Cook, Lisa Davenport, David Halperin, Victoria Kahn, and Nancy Logan.

I learned most of what I know about the English eighteenth century from Bliss Carnochan and Terry Castle. Their own work and their criticism of mine continue to provide me with a model for rigorous and graceful scholarship. The intellectual roots of my work also extend much further back, to Ken Sharpe's seminars about political theory and Susan Snyder's seminars about Renaissance literature at Swarthmore College, where I first began to learn to think.

When I was working on the early drafts of this project, I received financial and intellectual support from the English Department at Stanford University, the Stanford Humanities Center, and the Thomas Killefer Dissertation Fellowship. A Summer Fellowship from Mills College helped to support me while I completed the revisions.

M.K.

Narrative Transvestism

Introduction

The conventional history of the English novel begins with Defoe or Richardson in the early years of the eighteenth century and traces the genre through Fielding, with a sidelong glance at Sterne and Smollett, to Jane Austen.[1] Literary critics have relied on this version of the origin and development of the novel to generalize about the political position of these "fathers" of the English novel, about an unbroken line of novelistic tradition, and about the celebration of domestic stability and happiness that seemed to be built into both the literary tradition and the structure of the novel itself. The most compelling version of this argument is, of course, Ian Watt's *Rise of the Novel: Studies in Defoe, Richardson, and Fielding*;[2] since its publication in 1957 literary critics have positioned their arguments about the English novel in relation to Watt's. Those emendations and challenges to Watt's argument are finally beginning to change the way the

[1]I am explicitly concerned here with the origins of the English novel. The history of the novel in France or Spain presents certain obvious complications to this simple narrative. Bakhtin and other critics of comparative literature talk about the novel as a form that has been evolving since classical times. M. M. Bakhtin, *The Dialogic Imagination: Four Essays*, ed. Michael Holquist, trans. Caryl Emerson and Michael Holquist (Austin: University of Texas Press, 1981). I discuss Bakhtin's idea of heteroglossia at greater length when I elaborate my notion of narrative transvestism.

[2]Ian Watt, *The Rise of the Novel: Studies in Defoe, Richardson, and Fielding* (Berkeley: University of California Press, 1957).

English novel and its origins are treated both in works of criticism and in the classroom. They certainly inform this book, which was prompted by the fundamental question of much recent critical theory from deconstruction to feminist theory: What's been left out, and what was to be gained from leaving it out?

What has been left out of most criticism of individual English novels as well as of the history of the novel is any interpretation of the explosive fact that many of what we continue to cite as the first canonical novels (*Moll Flanders, Roxana, Pamela, Clarissa,* the not-quite-canonical *Fanny Hill*) were written by men in the person of women. I have developed the concept of narrative transvestism to describe this use by a male author of a first-person female narrator, and I use the concept to investigate how the eighteenth-century discourse about gender participates in the development of the narrative consciousness that became the distinguishing characteristic of the modern novel.

Women have also written novels using a first-person male persona, and it might seem appropriate to include such novels here. But the question, what does a woman author have to gain from using a man's voice? turns out not to be symmetrical to, what does a male author have to gain from using a woman's? Women are borrowing the voice of authority; men are seemingly abdicating it. The structure of real-world transvestism that I have used as a model for the structure of narrative transvestism may also be unsuitable for women. Most psychoanalytic descriptions of transvestism—which disagree in many other respects— agree that there is no such thing as a female transvestite. Women may dress as men, but they don't seem to do so as part of a cycle of reaffirming their feminine identity. Thus, while women authors have certainly experimented with the transgression of gender boundaries in fiction, it is the work of another book to see what, if any, aspects of the concept of narrative transvestism provide a useful model for analysis of those texts.

Recent work on the eighteenth-century novel has, of course, raised the issue of gender in a variety of ways, from explorations of the cultural and literary climate that determined what and how women could write, through discussions of the notion of "women's writing," to investigations of how gender and gender expectations have influenced critical responses to the novel. I am indebted to all these critical approaches, and I have borrowed something from each of them to form my concept of narrative transvestism.

Perhaps the most obvious challenge to the traditional literary canon and the assumptions it allows critics to make about literary interpretation comes from those who are trying to revise the canon itself. Critics including Dale Spender, Janet Todd, and Jane Spencer have questioned the omission of women novelists of the eighteenth century and have worked to restore their novels to print and to critical consciousness. Such critics detail the great success achieved by women writers such as Sarah Fielding, Aphra Behn, Delariviere Manley, Charlotte Lennox, and Fanny Burney while noting that this success was achieved against great odds and against the strong societal censure of "scribbling women," which eventually nudged these popular writers into obscurity. Plenty of women wrote both well and successfully in the eighteenth century, they argue, and the male novelists we now cite as the first were often responding to and learning from contemporary novels by women. The force of patriarchal literary history is such, however, that novels by women were relegated to the margins simply because their authors were by definition marginal. Restoring these works to the canon would allow us to hear the voice of the other side of the literary and cultural dialogue that produced the English novel.[3]

[3]Jane Spencer, *The Rise of the Woman Novelist: From Aphra Behn to Jane Austen* (New York: Basil Blackwell, 1986); Dale Spender, *Mothers of the Novel: 100 Good Women Writers before Jane Austen* (New York: Pandora, 1986); Janet Todd, *The Sign of Angellica: Women, Writing, and Fiction, 1660–1800* (New York: Columbia University Press, 1989). In an effort to be concise I have lumped Todd, Spender, and Spencer together, but of course their arguments are not identical and are considerably more subtle than I have space to delineate here. Briefly, Spender is concerned not so much with investigating why early fiction by women has been suppressed as with redressing the problem. Her book is a detailed catalogue of, as its subtitle states, "100 good women writers before Jane Austen." Todd's book situates the achievements of women writers within

A second recent critical trend comprises the less radical approach of extending and modifying the canon and the conventional view of the origins of the English novel to include the impact of history and politics upon literature as well as literary criticism. Among the most influential books in this category is Michael McKeon's *Origins of the English Novel, 1600–1740*, which posits that the novel was developed to negotiate institutional and epistemological uncertainty. McKeon argues that the novel epitomizes generic instability and thus can accommodate a new instability in the conceptual and explanatory paradigms that used to provide an authoritative structure for literature. Work by Nancy Armstrong, Terry Eagleton, John Bender, and others also attempts to persuade us of the importance of a newly conceived social and political context for the literature we are reading. Eagleton, in particular, and the others to a lesser extent stress that in addition to reading literature in a specific context, we also read it with specific social and political assumptions. Although some of these critics, notably Armstrong and Eagleton, consider the impact of gender on writing and reading, their primary interest is the impact of class and politics on the production and interpretation of literature.[4]

---

the cultural and historical developments of which she argues they were very much a part. Thus, while she details what she considers to be the female themes of "female signs and masks, as well as the social and moral effects of sexual desire and manipulation" (2), she stresses the women writers' responses to changes in society and society's changing evaluation of women writers from the Restoration to the late eighteenth century. Spencer argues most forcefully that eighteenth-century British society was particularly ripe for women novelists, not because the public position of women was improving, but because the novel addressed itself to society's attempts to limit women to the private and domestic sphere. She states that "the novel was exactly suited to bridging the gap between women and the public world" (20) because "women novelists were carving a public niche for themselves by recommending a private, domestic life for their heroines" (20), and because the novel drew on private—and therefore feminine—modes of writing such as "the familiar letter, the diary and the domestic conduct book" (20). Spencer thus posits a kind of dialectic between patriarchal pronouncements about women's authority existing only in the private sphere and the ambiguous public authority of women who published novels about that same private sphere.

[4]Michael McKeon, *The Origins of the English Novel, 1600–1740* (Baltimore: Johns Hopkins University Press, 1987). McKeon's emphasis on the ancient roots of the

My third category of challenges to traditional criticism of the novel is, like the first, explicitly feminist and, like the second, eager to find ways to reread the works in the traditional canon. These works bring to bear on the traditional canon an emphasis on changing notions of gender within the texts and within the societies that produced them and those that interpret them. The revelation that neither the definition nor the valuation of gender is fixed allows us to ask new questions about the ways texts both participate in and comment upon the social construction of gender. Sandra Gilbert and Susan Gubar's theories about the anxiety of female authorship, and their image of silent women historically "imprisoned in male texts . . . generated soley . . . by male expectations and designs,"[5] have been developed and challenged since their book was published in 1979, but, like Watt's work, theirs is the foundation upon which many later critical insights rest. In particular, Nancy Miller and Terry Castle have explored the semiotics of gender in eighteenth-century texts. Both these critics emphasize the struggle within these texts for control over a woman's story and its meaning.[6]

In proposing an explanation for the fact that so many early eighteenth-century novels purport to be women's autobiogra-

---

novel, along with his elaboration of a dialectic between history and the novel form, owes a great deal to Bakhtin. See also Nancy Armstrong, *Desire and Domestic Fiction: A Political History of the Novel* (New York: Oxford University Press, 1987); John Bender, *Imagining the Penitentiary: Fiction and the Architecture of Mind in Eighteenth-Century England* (Chicago: University of Chicago Press, 1987); and Terry Eagleton's work, especially *The Rape of Clarissa: Writing, Sexuality, and Class Struggle in Samuel Richardson* (Minneapolis: University of Minnesota Press, 1982) and *Literary Theory: An Introduction* (Minneapolis: University of Minnesota Press, 1983).

[5]Sandra M. Gilbert and Susan Gubar, *The Madwoman in the Attic: The Woman Writer and the Nineteenth-Century Literary Imagination* (New Haven: Yale University Press, 1979), p. 12.

[6]Nancy K. Miller, " 'I's' in Drag: The Sex of Recollection," *The Eighteenth Century: Theory and Interpretation*, 22 (Winter 1981): 47–57, and *The Heroine's Text: Readings in the French and English Novel, 1722–1782* (New York: Columbia University Press, 1980); Terry Castle, *Clarissa's Ciphers: Meaning and Disruption in Richardson's "Clarissa"* (Ithaca: Cornell University Press, 1982), *Masquerade and Civilization: The Carnivalesque in Eighteenth-Century English Culture and Fiction* (Stanford: Stanford University Press, 1986), and "Matters Not Fit to Be Mentioned: Fielding's *The Female Husband*," ELH 49 (Fall 1982): 602–22.

phies but were in fact written by men, I offer a theory of the novel as a form which allowed its authors to exploit the instability of gender categories and which is thus inseparable from its own continual reexamination and redefinition of those categories. The narrative consciousness that we have come to identify with the novel is always an explicitly gendered consciousness, although it is not fixed in either gender. It is not by accident, then, that the novels of Richardson and Defoe are thematically as well as structurally concerned with the creation of a gendered voice and with the transgression of gender boundaries.

Much has been made of the connection between confessional autobiography and the novel and of the new use in the eighteenth century of a first-person narrative for fiction. Critics have until recently, however, overlooked the circumstance that the male author's "autobiography" is voiced by a woman. No doubt they have done so in part because men have always assumed that it is perfectly natural for them to speak *for* women.[7] But authors such as Richardson and Defoe are also speaking *through* women, and they are in the process endowing that female voice with a great deal of power and receiving a different kind of power from it. I use the term "narrative transvestism" to refer to this process whereby a male author gains access to a culturally defined female voice and sensibility but runs no risk of being trapped in the devalued female realm. Through narrative transvestism the male author plays out, in the metaphorical body of the text, the ambiguous possibilities of identity and gender. I argue that this narrative projection of the male self into an imagined female voice and experience was an integral part of the emerging novel's radical and destabilizing investigation of how

[7]Elaine Showalter discusses the appropriation of feminist criticism by male critics in her article "Critical Cross-Dressing: Male Feminists and the Woman of the Year," *Raritan* 3 (Fall 1983): 130–49. She cites Robert Stoller on the transvestite's desire to create a phallic woman in support of her argument that male critics who don't see that their efforts to "read as a woman" might be problematic are simply erasing the woman from feminist criticism. Her point is well taken, although I am somewhat less sanguine about the power of this phallic woman since s/he must be continually recreated through the transvestite's (even the critical transvestite's) endless revelation and redisguising of the man beneath the womanly facade.

an individual creates an identity and, as our society if not our biology requires, a gendered identity.

Other critics have recently turned their attention to male authors' use of female narrators, but as will become clear, I define narrative transvestism and its effects rather differently from the "ventriloquism" or "appropriation" with which most of these critics are concerned.[8] Most of this work on the use of a female narrative persona by a male author has emphasized the hegemony of one gender over another. Eve Sedgwick and Nancy Miller, for example, speak of a homoerotic economy in which the female dummies are used as counters between male ventriloquists. Conversely, James Carson emphasizes the narrative power of the "dummies" and the critique of patriarchy that inheres in the choice of a female persona. It seems clear, however, that both approaches are correct but neither is ultimately true. The dynamic structure of transvestism reveals transvestism's inability to be fixed in either category despite its attempts to reaffirm once and for all the hegemony of the masculine.

I should briefly note that in my terminology sex and gender are two very distinct things, although they are, of course, intimately connected. Sex is a matter of biology (although biology turns out to be indecisive in some cases), and gender is a social and personal construct. Essentially, gender is the code of language, dress, thought, manners, and—often—sexual behavior that society deems acceptable from a person of one sex or the other. Gender, then, is the social overlay upon sex, and another gender (unlike another sex) can be assumed temporarily and then discarded.

"Narrative transvestism" is my conjunction of a literary term and a psychoanalytic one. Together they precisely define a realm

---

[8]These critics include Terry Castle, "Matters Not Fit to Be Mentioned"; Nancy K. Miller, " 'I's' in Drag"; Eve Kosofsky Sedgwick, *Between Men: English Literature and Male Homosocial Desire* (New York: Columbia University Press, 1985); and Elizabeth C. Goldsmith, ed., *Writing the Female Voice: Essays on Epistolary Literature* (Boston: Northeastern University Press, 1989), which includes the essay by James Carson, "Narrative Cross-Dressing and the Critique of Authorship in the Novels of Richardson" (pp. 95–113), to which I refer later in this paragraph.

within which it is possible to talk about the formal demands and constraints of gendered imaginations and gendered voices as eighteenth-century England constructed them. In Chapter 1 I situate a psychoanalytic description of transvestism within eighteenth-century discussions of gender, and I examine the ways in which the structure of narrative transvestism gave early male novelists access to the dangerous but valuable, irrational and seemingly unbounded female realm. In Chapter 2 I elaborate on the part that Defoe's narrative transvestism in *Roxana* plays in complicating that novel's thematic investigation of how one goes about creating an expressive self. Defoe teases his readers by hiding the "true" author of the book beneath the shifting layers of Roxana's confession, his editorial intervention, the unimpeachable truth of historical facts, and the seductive unreliability of fiction. His goal is to entice us into organizing Roxana's character and her narrative when she cannot—and, once enticed, we participate in Defoe's model of the construction of a self. In Chapter 3 I analyze Richardson's personal correspondence to show that he poses as the editor of his own letters just as he does of his fictional characters' letters in *Clarissa*. In the novel he carries this pose further to abdicate authorial control over his characters, only to reassert that authority as a privileged reader of his own works.

This book relies on work that other scholars have done to uncover the period's concepts of proper gender roles and the debate over the stability of those roles as it is shown in theories of male and female language, discussions of sexuality and medical speculation about sex changes, notions about clothing and the semiotics of dress, and domestic conduct books. All this work provides a context for my analysis of narrative transvestism in the novels of Richardson and Defoe. I offer an overview of that context in Chapter 1, but I do not rehearse each step in those historical and social analyses. The notes to that chapter provide direction for anyone who wants to pursue that part of the argument in greater depth. (And in an effort to keep the text uncluttered, I have in general relegated most of my discussion of critical debates to the notes.)

I was steered to these efforts to define the content of gender categories in the period in part by questions I received in response to early talks that I gave on this topic. I was often asked if I thought the narrative "she" created by the early English male novelists was in fact a believable woman and whether or not her "autobiography" could possibly be true to a real woman's experience of the world. Such questions have a noble critical heritage. In *The Rise of the Novel*, for example, Ian Watt takes note of and then dismisses Defoe's use of narrative transvestism in *Moll Flanders*:

> Moll Flanders, of course, has many feminine traits; she has a keen eye for fine clothes and clean linen, and shows a wifely concern for the creature comforts of her males. Further, the early pages of the book undoubtedly present a young girl with a lifelike clarity, and later there are many touches of a rough cockney humour that is undeniably feminine in tone. But these are relatively external and minor matters, and the essence of her character and actions is, to one reader at least, essentially masculine. This is a personal impression, and would be difficult, if not impossible, to establish: but it is at least certain that Moll accepts none of the disabilities of her sex, and indeed one cannot but feel that Virginia Woolf's admiration for her was largely due to admiration of a heroine who so fully realized one of the ideals of feminism: freedom from any involuntary involvment in the feminine role.[9]

At points in the trajectory of narrative transvestism, which moves from a poorly defined and insecure male editor through a female narrator who is expressive by virtue of her ersatz femininity and back to the newly affirmed power of the male author, Defoe's relationship to his narrator is certainly one of admiring identification. But to assert that this admiration defines the limits of his authorial control over his narrator is to mistake one stage for the entire process.

Watt criticizes Moll for not being a woman, but of course she isn't a woman: she is a male author's narrative device, and her "unfeminine" traits are important not because they destroy the

[9]Watt, *Rise of the Novel*, p. 113. The next citation is from p. 115.

illusion of the female narrator but because they draw attention to it. Similarly failing to distinguish between the author's manipulation of gender as a thematic issue and a structural device, Watt mistakes Moll's ambitions for Defoe's: "Defoe's identification with Moll Flanders was so complete that, despite a few feminine traits, he created a personality that was in essence his own."

One could debate many of Watt's assumptions here, but for the time being I want to point out only that they lead critical inquiry away from the intersection of gender and narrative structure that we find in narrative transvestism. Indeed, they dismiss such concerns by simply stating that Moll was not a real woman and that Defoe's inability to create a real woman was one of the many signs of his incompetence as a novelist.

Although considerable attention is now being paid to narrative devices by which men write through women, much of it still focuses on this issue of whether or not a man can create a believable women in narrative, or vice versa. What became clear to me, however, as I read about various essentialist definitions of male and female, about operations to turn little boys into little girls and back again, and about historical evidence that human sexuality is not defined by "heterosexual" and "homosexual" but rather exists in each individual on a continuum between the two, is that the content of these categories is not nearly as important as the existence of the categories themselves. That is, male and female—however else they are defined—are always defined as opposites. Thus, the most incisive question we can pose about a male author's use of a female narrative voice is not, did he create a believable woman? but, what did he have to gain from the attempt? What is the point of creating a rather elaborate narrative structure to gain access to a voice on the other side of the structural divide between genders?

The answers to these questions lie, I believe, in the structure of transvestism itself, particularly in the transvestite's refusal to be defined by one gender or the other. Before I elaborate my understanding of the psychology of real-world transvestism and of how it is a useful tool for the analysis of the structure of the novel, however, I want to make clear what the aims of this book are, and what they are not. I do not intend to explore the sexual biographies of various eighteenth-century English authors but rather to investigate how the eighteenth-century discourse of gender and a new upheaval in the categories of male and female participate in the novel's narrative consciousness. In particular, the double-hinged structure of narrative transvestism, which highlights both the thematics of gender within the novel and the transgression and reaffirmation of those categories of gender in the narrative, points to an authorial awareness that has usually been denied to the early novelists. For example, when Richardson adds narrative transvestism to the epistolary form in *Pamela* and *Clarissa,* he is deliberately engaging his readers in an interplay between the truth or genuineness of the male editorial apparatus and the truth of the female letters themselves that precisely mirrors the transvestite's playfulness with, yet adherence to, rigid gender definitions. I concentrate here on the uses to which Richardson and Defoe put the rhetorical strategy of narrative transvestism and the ways our awareness of that strategy changes our readings of the novels.

Psychoanalytic theory about, and clinical and historical evidence of, transvestism can provide a model for understanding certain rhetorical strategies employed by the early English novelists; they do not provide me with clues to a buried pathology. "Transvestism" as applied to literary structures is not a diagnosis but a metaphor: it furnishes helpful analogies to the structures that govern an essentially literary masquerade, and it directs our attention to the dialectic of display and concealment exhibited by these eighteenth-century texts—to the complex negotiations between self and other that structure both the novelist's art and the reader's response. Similarly, my concern with the categories of male and female in the period is not an attempt to fix their content but rather an examination of what the insistence on such categories might mean, why an author would transgress their boundaries, and what impact that transgression had on the form and thematics of the novel.

I am writing about the eighteenth-century English novel, but this book is about something that neither ended nor began with the eighteenth century. The instability of gender categories that I detail was not unique to that period, although it was strikingly and constantly articulated then, and the attempt to mediate that instability by creating a riskily unstable but nevertheless enabling transvestite self is unique here only in that it produced the narrative structure that formed the basis of the novel. That narrative transvestite self is not in any sense the "true" self of the author; it is rather a provisional writing self, a stance from which the author can play with the instability that might otherwise immobilize him. I rely on Freudian theory and the revisions to that theory provided by the object relations school of psychoanalysis not because Freud somehow discovered a truth about sexuality applicable to people in all times and places but because he gave voice in a memorable way to certain preoccupations and anxieties of men in a patriarchal culture—one whose basic structure despite many changes has persisted since before the eighteenth century to the present. I am concerned with the politics of gender, not of sexuality, and those politics seem to revolve around the same issues in most societies and most periods.[10]

[10]See, for example, David Halperin, *One Hundred Years of Homosexuality: And Other Essays on Greek Love* (New York: Routledge, 1990), especially the essay "Why Is Diotima a Woman?", pp. 113–52, and John J. Winkler, *The Constraints of Desire: The Anthropology of Sex and Gender in Ancient Greece* (New York: Routledge, 1989).

1

Transvestism and Narrative Structures in Eighteenth-Century England

A transvestite is a man who dresses temporarily and periodically as a woman. He is not a transsexual who wants to *be* a woman and who today can be one, through surgery. Neither is he, generally, a homosexual. He is a heterosexual man who reaffirms his masculinity by dressing as a woman. In that dress, he does not become a woman; he becomes a man who is hiding his penis beneath his skirt. This is, of course, a simplistic formulation; obviously the essence of masculinity is not the penis, nor is it possible to reduce womanliness to a skirt. Similarly, while the transvestite can participate to some extent in the female realm, he never really creates a female body—only the illusion of one. The tools of this illusion are, however, the most obvious and powerful symbols the transvestite has at his disposal in his attempts to negotiate between the socially constructed extremes of gender difference. It is easy to become as preoccupied as the transvestite himself with the temporary success of the elaborate female costume. It is important to remember, however, that the costume is not really complete until it is revealed as a costume; the transvestite cross-dresses to undress. The cross-dressing, no matter how elaborate, is not the goal; rather, it is part of the process of creating a male self.[1]

[1]For my description of modern real-world transvestism, I have relied primarily on the work of Peter Ackroyd, Richard F. Docter, Deborah Feinbloom, and Robert

Transvestism does not involve any permanent alteration of the body whatsoever. On the contrary, the transvestite is enacting a fiction of gender transformation and directing his audience toward an inherently contradictory interpretation of his gender. Transvestism temporarily suspends the rules of logical consistency. The transvestite is a woman *and* he is a man. He is a woman while he is dressed, and he reveals himself as a man when he undresses. The impermanence of the transvestite self is crucial to its meaning and to its power. The man masquerading as a woman at a party, for example, knows himself to be within the social category of women without being of that category. Depending on the extent to which he makes clues to his biological sex a part of his masquerade, the transvestite may be inviting his audience to share in the incongruities of his masquerade, or he may be falsely presenting himself as a person of uncomplicated gender.

The social phenomenon of cross-dressing has, of course, existed in every society since ancient times,[2] but the term "transvestism" is a creation of the nineteenth century and its precise clinical meaning was in great dispute up to the 1950s. Even today

---

Stoller. My theoretical approach owes more to the work of the object relations theorists (such as D. W. Winnicott) and their concept of "gender relief" than to the work of Freud and his followers, who emphasize the role of transvestism as a route to genital satisfaction. I have also found Thomas Ogden's work on projective identification particularly useful for my conception of the structure of the transvestite's relation to the other. See Peter Ackroyd, *Dressing Up: Transvestism and Drag, the History of an Obsession* (New York: Simon and Schuster, 1979); Richard F. Docter, *Transvestites and Transsexuals: Toward a Theory of Cross-Gender Behavior* (New York: Plenum Press, 1988); Deborah Feinbloom, *Transvestites and Transsexuals: Mixed Views* (New York: Delacorte Press/Seymour Lawrence, 1975); Thomas H. Ogden, *Projective Identification and Psychotherapeutic Technique* (New York: Jason Aronson, 1982); Robert J. Stoller, *Sex and Gender*, vol. I: *The Development of Masculinity and Feminity* (New York: Jason Aronson, 1968, rpt. 1974); D. W. Winnicott, *Through Paediatrics to Psycho-Analysis* (New York: Basic Books, 1958, rpt. 1975).

[2]Ackroyd's *Dressing Up* provides a good introduction to the study of transvestism through history and across cultures. See also the essays in *Western Sexuality: Practice and Precept in Past and Present Times*, ed. Philippe Ariès and André Béjin (London: Basil Blackwell, 1985), in Halperin, *One Hundred Years of Homosexuality*, in Winkler, *Constraints of Desire*, and in *Sexual Underworlds of the Enlightenment*, ed. G. S. Rousseau and Roy Porter (Manchester: Manchester University Press, 1987).

it (like most psychoanalytic terms) is used differently by analysts and clinicians of different psychoanalytic schools.

The Structure of Transvestism

Although there are earlier catalogues of types of sexuality that include references to transvestites, Havelock Ellis was the first to make a genuine psychological study of the phenomenon. In his *Studies in the Psychology of Sex*, he cited the use of the term by Magnus Hirschfeld and immediately protested that it was inaccurate because it emphasized the change of clothes over what he considered to be the true symptom, which was the presence of a female aesthetic sense in a male body.[3] Ellis favored changing the name to either "eonism" (after the Chevalier d'Éon, whose story I detail later in this chapter) or "sexo-aesthetic inversion." With this proposed change Ellis implicitly recognized that the actual cross-dressing was a relatively unimportant part of a larger emotional structure. This recognition marks one of his differences from both Freud and Karl Abraham, who define transvestism in more limited terms as a psychosexual disturbance.[4] Other theorists have stressed the sexually charged nature of the transvestite's clothing fetish, but Ellis claims that the transvestite or eonist has a weak sex drive and that what drive he has is directed toward a version of himself instead of toward a true other.[5]

> The subject of the anomaly is not merely experiencing an inversion of general tastes in the sexual sphere; he has really attained to a specifically aesthetic emotional attitude in that sphere. In his admiration of the beloved he is not content to confine himself to the

[3]Havelock Ellis, *Studies in the Psychology of Sex*, Vol. III, Part II (New York: Random House, 1936). The article on eonism is in Part II, *Eonism and Other Supplementary Studies*. Hirschfeld's study was *Sexual Anomalies and Perversions*.
[4]Ellis explicitly marks this difference in *Studies in the Psychology of Sex*, 3:16.
[5]Since the use of the term "other" in its psychoanalytic and structural context has become so common in literary criticism, I have not capitalized it.

normal element of *Einfühlung* [empathy]; he adopts the whole aesthetic attitude by experiencing also the impulse of imitation. He achieves a completely emotional identification which is sexually abnormal but aesthetically correct. At the same time we may carry this conception beyond the aesthetic field into that of the psychic life generally. Such a conception has, for instance, been worked out by Prandtl. "Every 'you,'" says Prandtl, "every person outside myself, proceeds from a splitting up of myself, and is part of my own me." The Eonist thus becomes simply a person in whom a normal and even quite ordinary and inevitable process of thought is carried to an undue and abnormal length. He has put too much of "me" into the "you" that attracts him.[6]

The contention that "every 'you' . . . proceeds from a splitting up of myself, and is a part of my own me" is particularly resonant for the narcissism implied by what Ellis defines as the aesthetic component of transvestism. The transvestite engages in a kind of gender megalomania when he annexes every female "you" as part of "my own [male] me." He imitates a perceived other and thus makes her a part of himself. He can then adore this ersatz other without being frightened by her difference from him. Simply put, the transvestite man is engaged in creating the perfect woman. Ellis stresses that this is an aesthetic activity; Freud stresses that it is a libidinal one. But they agree on the narcissism involved and on the paradoxical structure of transvestism.

Any Freudian investigation of transvestism is complicated by a long psychoanalytic tradition of regarding all femininity as a masquerade. If womanliness is in fact a masquerade, then men have equal access to it, and the activity of the transvestite becomes at least as legitimate as that of any woman also learning to dress, walk, and make up her face as if she were a woman. I do not have space here to explore fully the implications of these branches of psychoanalytic theory for my treatment of transvestism. Clearly, however, if womanliness is itself merely masquer-

[6]Ellis, *Studies in the Psychology of Sex*, 3:107–8. Also on p. 108, Ellis claims that "The Eonist frequently shows feebleness of physical sexual impulse."

ade, then the transvestite's masquerade as not only a woman but a phallic woman turns the psychoanalytic screw once more.

Erving Goffman rather strikingly betrays our cultural confusion about whether womanliness is natural or a masquerade, and about whether or not it is possible to remain a woman if one is capable in so-called masculine realms, in a footnote to his *Stigma: Notes on the Management of Spoiled Identity*. In a discussion of what he calls "reverse passing," which he defines as passing as less qualified than one is, he remarks:

> I knew of a physician who was careful to refrain from using external symbols of her status, such as car-license tags, her only evidence of profession being an identification carried in her wallet. When faced with a public accident in which medical service was already being rendered the victim, or in which the victim was past helping, she would, upon examining the victim at a distance from the circle around him, quietly go her way without announcing her competence. In these situations she was what might be called a female impersonator.[7]

This last sentence is, of course, a paradoxical assertion, which reveals more about the inadequacy of gender categories than about the nature of womanliness. The transvestite exploits this same inadequacy, even though he seems to be wedded to the most simplistic definitions of gender. Indeed, a man who sometimes dresses as a woman might in fact be the literal embodiment of paradox itself. For, like the paradoxist, the transvestite does not commit himself. He asserts that something both is and is not true at the same time. For example, the transvestite simultaneously asserts that he is a better "woman" than anyone born

[7]Erving Goffman, *Stigma: Notes on the Management of Spoiled Identity* (Englewood Cliffs, N.J.: Prentice-Hall, 1963), p. 38. For a discussion of the issues of womanliness and masquerade, see Joan Rivière, "Womanliness as Masquerade," and Stephen Heath, "Joan Rivière and the Masquerade," in *Formations of Fantasy*, ed. V. Berguin (New York: Methuen, 1986), p. 35–44, and 45–61, as well as Jessica Benjamin, "A Desire of One's Own: Psychoanalytic Feminism and Intersubjective Space," and Mary Russo, "Female Grotesques: Carnival and Theory," in *Feminist Studies/Critical Studies*, ed. Teresa de Lauretis (Bloomington: Indiana University Press, 1986), pp. 78–101 and 213–29.

with female genitalia and that he is a man of essential masculinity. But both things can be true only while he continues the
cycle of dressing and undressing. Similarly, a paradox is both
true and untrue by virtue of its perpetual motion. As Rosalie
Colie writes in her book on paradox: "In more than one sense,
paradox equivocates. It lies, and it doesn't. It tells the truth, and
it doesn't. . . . [I]ts negative and positive meanings are so balanced that one meaning can never outweigh the other, though
weighted to eternity . . . its meanings [are] infinitely mirrored,
infinitely reflected in each other."[8]

In transvestism the self is split into a doubly gendered being
which "infinitely mirror[s]" itself. And this mirror image creates
an endless oscillation between the object and the reflection of the
object, a kind of infinite regress of self-absorption. In a mirror,
the transvestite can admire his female reflection while knowing
himself to be reassuringly male.[9] Not surprisingly mirrors, photographs of the male self in drag, and social proof of the effectiveness of the cross-dressing ("passing") are tremendously important for the transvestite.

The costumed gazer's temporary transfer of identity from the
physical self to the transforming reflection is a model of the
crucial movement in transvestism: the *temporary* assertion of a
female self whose very ephemeral nature enables the reassertion
of a masculine identity.

This transvestite model of a dynamic identity, or of contradictory meanings existing in an uneasy but balanced tension, is
very similar to one of Freud's central contentions: that the psyche is capable of adhering absolutely to two absolutely contradictory beliefs.[10] Thus, although Freud actually paid scant attention to transvestism in his writings aside from a few brief

[8]Rosalie L. Colie, *Paradoxia Epidemica: The Renaissance Tradition of Paradox* (Princeton: Princeton University Press, 1966), p. 6. She elaborates on p. 8: "Once more,
then, paradoxes turn out to be paradoxical, to do two things at once, two things
which contradict or cancel one another."

[9]Feinbloom, *Transvestites and Transsexuals*, pays particular attention to the importance of mirrors and photographs.

[10]See, for example, Sigmund Freud, "The Antithetical Sense of Primal Words"
(1910), in *Character and Culture*, ed. Philip Rieff (New York: Macmillan, 1963), pp. 44–

mentions of the subject in his *Three Essays on Sexuality*, he explored its structure in many different realms.[11]

Before I examine Freud's elaboration of the dynamic and paradoxical structure of transvestism in his book on Leonardo da Vinci, I want to pause to explicate my own use of Freudian theory. As I stated in the Introduction, I do not claim that Freud discovered a transhistorical truth about either sexuality (which in any case doesn't interest me as much as the social expression of gender) or the nature of the individual. I borrow from Freudian terms and theories precisely because Freud so powerfully articulated the patriarchal concept of masculine self and female other that is crucial to the process of transvestism—in the real world or in narrative. I argue that narrative transvestism allowed Defoe and Richardson to create provisional writing selves. These selves are not in any sense "true" selves but fruitful illusions of self-knowledge and self-presence; they are the effect of a complicated response to debates about gender in the period. I have borrowed the vocabulary of the object relations school for my descriptions of what the transvestite stands to gain from projecting parts of himself into the phallic woman he creates. This notion of temporary and self-protective projection is crucial to my idea that narrative transvestism—far from being a fully worked out strategy—was a kind of happy accident for Defoe and Richardson, who could achieve self-presence only in a realm from which they could, if necessary, beat a hasty retreat, and self-knowledge only when they had temporarily assumed a female persona.[12]

---

50. On p. 44 he quotes his own *Interpretation of Dreams:* "The attitude of dreams towards the category of antithesis and contradiction is most striking. This category is simply ignored; the word 'No' does not seem to exist for a dream. Dreams show a special tendency to reduce two opposites to a unity or to represent them as one thing."

[11]Sigmund Freud, *Three Essays on the Theory of Sexuality* (1905), trans. James Strachey (New York: Avon Books, 1962).

[12]For descriptions from the object relations school of the formation of gender identity, see Ogden, *Projective Identification,* and Winnicott, *Through Paediatrics to Psycho-Analysis.*

In general, there are now two psychoanalytic approaches to the issue of transvestism. The first, based on Freud's theories, concentrates on the cross-dressing as the

In the next section I more fully describe various crises of epistemology and the concomitant blurring of gender boundaries in eighteenth-century England and the resulting attempts by various parts of society to redefine and codify gender categories. This exploration of the categories of masculine and feminine in eighteenth-century English society and novels is not an attempt to fix the content of those categories. I want rather to examine what the simultaneous insistence on and transgression of the boundaries of those categories might mean. Thus the Lacanian and feminist revisions of the Freudian notions of masculine and feminine are, while fascinating, not precisely relevant to this study. I am, however, indebted to many of these recent challenges to Freud for freeing me from the lingering power of essentialist notions about the content or value of gender categories.[13] And once I saw that the relationship between the categories was more important than the content of either one, I was able to make the conceptual link between real-world transvestism and narrative transvestism that governs this book. In discussing Freud's analysis of the Mona Lisa, I show why transvestism is a useful conceptual model for an analysis of the early English novels in which a male author abandons himself to a culturally defined female voice and sensibility, but only temporarily, and only within an encompassing literary structure in

---

means to libidinal or genital satisfaction. The second, which stems from the work of the English object relations school, stresses the concept of gender relief. For my work, the concept of gender relief is more important. I do not deny the libidinal component of real-world transvestism, but since I am reading literary texts (not psychoanalyzing real-world transvestites), the emphasis on gender stereotypes and the temporary transgression of them is more useful.

[13]For books on the Lacanian and feminist challenges to Freud, see Charles Bernheimer and Claire Kahane, eds., In Dora's Case: Freud-Hysteria-Feminism (New York: Columbia University Press, 1985); Nancy Chodorow, The Reproduction of Mothering: Psychoanalysis and the Sociology of Gender (Berkeley: University of California Press, 1978); Shoshana Felman, ed., Literature and Psychoanalysis: The Question of Reading Otherwise (Baltimore: Johns Hopkins University Press, 1982); Jane Gallop, The Daughter's Seduction: Feminism and Psychoanalysis, (Ithaca: Cornell University Press, 1982); and Jacques Lacan, Écrits: A Selection, trans. Alan Sheridan (New York: W. W. Norton, 1977). For an argument (on which I rely in the next section) about the social construction of both sexuality and gender, see Michel Foucault, The History of Sexuality, vol. I: An Introduction (New York: Vintage Books, 1980).

which he edits, annotates, or otherwise directs the reader's interpretation of his woman's narrative.

In his book on Leonardo da Vinci, Freud deals at length with the contradictory impulses that give Leonardo's art its complexity and its genius. And, like Ellis, Freud explicitly links the creative or aesthetic sense to the artist's refusal to be limited by the boundaries of traditional definitions of gender.

Freud begins with what he sees as the problem of "the stain of unsteadiness" on Leonardo's reputation.[14] Citing Leonardo's great dedication to and absorption in his art, Freud is puzzled by this mystery about Leonardo's "flightiness" (11) and by the similarly conventional wisdom that Leonardo's art itself is deeply mysterious. He takes as his test case an analysis of the Mona Lisa because Leonardo "worked for years on the portrait of Mona Lisa, the wife of the Florentine, de Gioconda, without being able to bring it to completion" (11), and because this picture in which Walter Pater sees "the embodiment of the entire erotic experience of modern man, . . . the ideal lady" (80–81) was painted by an artist of whom Freud contends, "[T]he storming passions of the soul-stirring and consuming kind, in which others experience the best part of their lives, seem to have missed him" (22).

Freud centers his analysis of Leonardo's relation to his art on a memory or fantasy that Leonardo recorded in his scientific notebooks:

It seems that it had been destined before that I should occupy myself so thoroughly with the vulture, for it comes to my mind as a very early memory, when I was still in the cradle, a vulture came down to me, opened my mouth with his tail and struck me many times with his tail against my lips. (33–34)

For Freud, this fantasy contains representations of all Leonardo's sexual and emotional ambiguity. In particular, because Leonardo's role in the fantasy is an entirely passive one, Freud

[14]Sigmund Freud, *Leonardo da Vinci: A Study in Psychosexuality,* trans. A. A. Brill (New York: Random House, 1916), p. 2. Future page references are in parentheses in the text.

attributes to Leonardo a strong identification with women—specifically with the nursing mother for whom he takes the vulture to be a stand-in. As he traverses the layers of meaning in this fantasy, however, Freud comes to a more complicated analysis. He sees in the vulture a representation of the phallic mother, and he links this representation of what he calls a "third sex" (63) to ancient myths of androgynous deities. He sees these deities as symbolic—like Leonardo's fantasy—of the union of the masculine and the feminine that is necessary for all creation.[15]

> Mythology may also offer the explanation that the phallus which was added to the feminine body was meant to denote the creative primitive force of nature, and all these hermaphroditic deistic formations express the idea that only a union of the masculine and feminine elements can result in a worthy representation of divine perfection. . . . The infantile assumption of the maternal penis is thus the common source of origin for the androgynous formation of the maternal deities like the Egyptian goddess *Mut* and the vulture's "coda" (tail) in Leonardo's childhood phantasy. (53, 58)[16]

Freud discusses Leonardo's homosexuality in the context of this fantasy of a phallic mother/goddess who represents a "third sex," and he suggests that Leonardo's anxieties about allying himself with one or another of the components of this third sex fueled his art and its mysteries.

From here Freud returns to the Mona Lisa and to her "remarkably fascinating and puzzling smile" (75). He identifies the puzzle as the presence of "two diverse elements . . . united in the smile of Mona Lisa" (76). Freud cites several contradictory in-

---

[15]See especially chap. 3, pp. 50–73.

[16]See also pp. 53–54: "When the male child first directs his curiosity to the riddle of the sexual life, he is dominated by the interest for his own genitals. He finds this part of the body too valuable and too important to believe that it would be missing in other persons to whom he feels such a resemblance. As he cannot divine that there is still another equally valuable type of genital formation he must grasp the assumption that all persons, also women, possess such a member as he. This preconception is so firm in the youthful investigator that it is not destroyed even by the first observation of the genitals in little girls."

terpretations of this smile: "the very essence of femininity: the tenderness and coquetry, the modesty and quiet voluptuousness . . . a royal calmness, her instincts of conquest, of ferocity, the entire heredity of the species, the will of seduction and ensnaring. . . . Good and evil, cruelty and compassion, graceful and cat-like she laughed" (77–78) and then declines to resolve the contradiction, stating instead that the contradiction is essential to the smile's mystery and to its power. He notes that Leonardo was as captivated by the contradiction as his audience: "her smile fascinated the artist no less than all spectators for these 400 years. . . . He transferred these features, especially the mysterious smile and the peculiar glance, to all faces which he later painted or drew" (79, 80).

Leonardo's inability to complete the Mona Lisa and his compulsion to paint that smile over and over again become for Freud evidence that Leonardo's "mother possessed that mysterious smile which he lost" (82) and that in the Mona Lisa, Leonardo "represented the wish fulfillment of the boy infatuated with his mother in such a blissful union of the male and female nature" (89). This passage is very clearly a description of the cycle of transvestism enacted in paint instead of with clothing. When Freud notes that in the model for the painting Leonardo saw something of himself, the link becomes even more suggestive. If the portrait of the Mona Lisa functioned as a kind of mirror for Leonardo, then the fact that the portrait remained unfinished becomes even more compelling: like the transvestite needing to see his male and female selves reflected at the same time, Leonardo may have been layering his female self-portrait over his male self-portrait in the Mona Lisa. And if he was to achieve the identity and the creative power he sought in this representation of himself as a third sex, the process could never be completed. Stopping at either gendered pole would mean being defined by its limitations rather than having access, in the "union of the masculine and feminine elements," to "a worthy representation of divine perfection" (53).

Curiously, Freud suggests that Leonardo was painting a self-

portrait by refusing to assert that it was a self-portrait: "As Leonardo's Mona Lisa was a portrait, we cannot assume that he has
added to her face a trait of his own, so difficult to express, which
she herself did not possess" (79). With this negative formulation
Freud seems to be saying that Leonardo found a trait in this
woman's features that was so like his own that he was able to
paint a self-portrait that was also a portrait of someone else. By
painting her essential femininity he also painted or created his
own masculinity. She is himself and his mother in a "blissful
union of the male and female nature" (89). The mystery of
gender in the Mona Lisa is also for Leonardo a mystery of
identity, and Freud sees Leonardo's fascination with her "enig-
matic smile" and his "wavering between art and science" (116) as
parts of his efforts to create an identity that could encompass that
mystery of gender rather than resolving it into its component
and unsatisfactory parts.

In the last pages of his study Freud anticipates the "criticism of
even friends and adepts of psychoanalysis, that I have only
written a psychoanalytic romance" (116) by pointing out the
limitations of psychoanalysis and biology alike. He nicely implies, however, that psychoanalytic romance is the only route
to understanding "artistic attainment"—the romance is simply
contained within one psyche; it is a process in which "a splitting
up of myself" helps to create "my own me."[17] According to
Freud, even biology follow this model: "Biological investigation
of our time endeavors to explain the chief traits of the organic
constitution of a person through the fusion of male and female
predispositions in the material sense" (119–20).

This reference to material evidence—and indeed Freud's entire analysis of the Mona Lisa—has recently been given further
resonance by material evidence of a different sort. In 1987 Lillian Schwartz used a computer to superimpose Leonardo's only
known self-portrait (a drawing in red chalk of himself in old age)
upon the Mona Lisa. She discovered that

[17]Ellis, *Studies in the Psychology of Sex*, 3:108.

the relative locations of the nose, mouth, chin, eyes and forehead in one precisely matched the other. Merely flipping up the corner of the mouth would produce the mysterious smile, and a reduction of the pouch under Leonardo's eye is all that is necessary to match the Mona Lisa's horizontal lid. When measurements were taken, it was found that the distance between the inner canthi, the inner corners of the eyes—one of the most strikingly individual measurements in a face—deviated by less than 2 percent. . . . Artist and model were one and the same. The Mona Lisa is Leonardo da Vinci's portrait of himself.[18]

Schwartz backs up her claim by noting that "for Leonardo, the world was a collection of hidden metaphors [and . . .] optical paradoxes; even his handwriting was reversed and legible only when held up to a mirror" (50–52). She adds that we have only rumors on which to base our assumption that a real woman sat for the portrait and that, contrary to Leonardo's usually meticulous records, "no trace of a commission, payments, or preliminary studies for the Mona Lisa has ever come to light" (52). Moreover, Leonardo took the painting with him on his travels and worked on it at intervals for almost fifteen years. She concludes that Leonardo was not painting "the likeness of a real person at all," but that "indulging his love of ambiguity, his penchant for riddles, he created a complex mythological, allegorical work, in which contrasts of life and death, light and darkness, male and female, barrenness and fertility play across the image" (52).[19]

The model for this mythological work was himself, "occasionally projected into the painting . . . transformed by narcissistic memory back into his handsome, beardless young manhood"

[18]Lillian Schwartz, "Leonardo's Mona Lisa," *Art and Antiques* (January 1987): 50. Further references are in parentheses in the text.

[19]Schwartz further notes that the figure has often been described as androgynous with its absence of jewelry, its unfashionable dress, its oversized arms and shoulders, and so on. "One suggestion that crops up again and again in the literature on the painting is that Leonardo did paint the Mona Lisa from life, but used a male for the model" (53).

(54). Schwartz cites further material evidence for her claim,[20] all of which fits nicely within the structure that Freud identified as the self's search for a creative identity. I have further characterized the structure Freud describes—in which the self continually shifts its identity from male to female and back again to claim the attributes of both and the limitations of neither—as transvestism. Leonardo's "occasional projection of himself" into the Mona Lisa was his enactment of this same process.

For the thing that most strikingly differentiates transvestism from the many things with which it has often been confused (transsexualism, homosexual drag, etc.) is its compulsively cyclical nature. The transvestite wants only *temporarily* to feel like a woman. His cross-dressing serves to emphasize for him his essential manhood and his difference from women. Thus the cross-dressing's periodicity is crucial to its success. In fact, the whole nature of transvestism—its reason for being—is that it can embrace contradiction *over time.*

Robert Stoller's description of the transvestite's psychic process emphasizes that the phallic woman whose form Freud finds in ancient myths and sculptures can only exist while the transvestite process continues. Thus the transvestite's identity as one who can control the phallic woman who created him by becoming a better phallic woman depends upon continual contradiction and movement.

A man with a sense of being feminine while cross-dressing is excitedly aware of being a male. Essential to his perversion are the

[20]Such evidence includes an analysis of the knots along the neckline of the Mona Lisa's dress. These were of a sort that particularly fascinated Leonardo, and Schwartz takes them to be one of the painter's habitual clues to the identity of his subject. She sums up: "Leonardo's use of himself resolves the problem of the existence of a model who was available over a period of years in different locations within a small household known to contain no women. It accounts for the dress, the lack of identifying jewelry, and the singular characteristics of the posture. It is consistent with the absence of records and sketches, the lack of allusions to the picture throughout the unusually long period of time spent painting it. It explains the use of the veil and the sfumato technique to deliberately merge forms, outlines, the corners of the eyes and mouth into soft shadows" (54).

two aspects of gender identity: the later one, *I am feminine,* and the earlier core identity, *I am (nonetheless) a male.* . . .

He has identified with a "phallic" woman (mother) and consciously senses himself to be a phallic "woman." He therefore can tell himself that he is, or with practice will become, a better woman than a biological female if he chooses to do so.[21]

The acting out of transvestism is a continual play between the extremes of gender stereotypes. That is, the process of dressing up as the most womanly woman to reinforce one's essential manhood actually reasserts the socially constructed extremes of gender difference, even though it temporarily clouds them. As Stoller puts it: "Transvestism is in great part a defensive structure raised to protect a threatened but desired sense of mas-

---

[21]Stoller, *Sex and Gender,* p. 40 and p. 117. All emphases are Stoller's. Stoller's work as a whole is marked by a certain simplistic misogynistic Freudianism so that, although he asks fascinating questions about gender and sexuality, his conclusions often seem oddly out of kilter. I have relied on his descriptions of the behavior of transvestites while questioning the conclusions he has drawn from his own observations. As one example of his disconcerting habit (which is in evidence in all of his work) of leaping from insightful observations to simplistic psychoanalytic conclusions, I offer one more quotation from *Sex and Gender:* "In his classic paper on transvestism, Fenichel points to the importance of the concept of the phallic woman as an invention of the transvestite, a fantasy he must create as a protection against his fear of castration during the oedipal phase. I would like to state this a little more fully: The transvestite, his sense of wholeness and worth in himself damaged, often *before* the oedipal phase, by the powerful feminizing effect of the woman who dressed him [in girl's clothes] or who otherwise scorned his maleness, has a disturbance in his sense of identity, in his taken-for-granted feeling of wholeness as a male. Because of this, he senses that that prime *insignia* of maleness, his penis, is in danger. Then, knowing of the biological and social "inferiority" of women, and also knowing that within himself there is a propensity toward being reduced to this "inferior" state, he denies that such creatures exist and invents the "phallic" woman. In a way, he does not have to invent such a person, for the living prototype actually has existed in his life—that is, the fiercely dangerous and powerful woman who already has humiliated him as a child. But he will have his triumph over her and all women, in the process of which he will reestablish his masculinity, the scar of the perversion remaining as a permanent sign of the original traumatic relationship. While it seems paradoxical, this triumph comes when he dresses up as a woman, for then, appearing like a woman, he can nonetheless say that he is a whole person, since he is the living proof that there is such a thing as a woman who has a penis. Transvestites often express this quite consciously in their statement that with a little practice they can get to be a better woman than any woman is, since they possess the best of both man and woman" (215).

culinity and maleness, and the corollary, to preserve a badly threatened potency. One should not be fooled by the apparent paradox that he does this via the detour of dressing like a woman."[22]

Ackroyd also notes that transvestism "implicitly adher[es] to the prevailing sexual and social codes."[23] That adherence to those polar extremes of gender delineates the realm in which the transvestite can safely and suggestively transgress boundaries.[24]

The real-world transvestite is reassured that his costume is always only a costume. In terms of gender, the transvestite can assert that he is a woman and then demonstrate that he is not. Within the magic narcissistic circle whose circumference is bounded by the constantly reinforced images of real man and real woman, nothing is fixed. And, in psychoanalytic terms, the phallic woman, that all-powerful being, can exist after all.[25]

[22]Stoller, *Sex and Gender*, p. 180.

[23]Ackroyd, *Dressing Up*, p. 14. It is worth citing the entire passage in which Ackroyd differentiates homosexuality from transvestism. I don't agree with him that transvestism is ultimately not misogynistic, but its misogyny is certainly of a complicated and ambiguous sort. "It is also necessary to distinguish transvestism from drag because, although there are connections to be traced between the two phenomena, they remain fundamentally separate. Drag is primarily a homosexual performance; most transvestites are heterosexual, often married and with children. Again drag may be a publicly acceptable way for certain homosexual transvestites to relieve their obsession, but instead of implicitly adhering to the prevailing sexual and social codes, as transvestism does, it flouts and breaks them. Drag parodies and mocks women—it is misogynistic both in origin and in intent, which transvestism clearly is not. The contemporary male transvestite wishes to create at least the illusion of femininity—"to pass" as a woman, either publicly or privately. For him, female clothes are a serious expression of fetishistic or anarchic tendencies. They are not a vehicle for satire at women's expense."

[24]Natalie Zemon Davis, in *Society and Culture in Early Modern France* (Stanford: Stanford University Press, 1975), claims that "festive and literary inversions in sex roles . . . served to reinforce hierarchical structure [but] literary and festive inversion in preindustrial Europe was a product not just of stable hierarchy but also of changes in the location of power and property, so this inversion could prompt new ways of thinking about the system and reacting to it" (142–43). Peter Ackroyd also cites many examples of transvestism as both symbolic of and enabling for political upheaval.

[25]In this context it is interesting to note that most psychoanalytic theories now agree that transvestism is an entirely male phenomenon. Freud stated that women could not be transvestites because the transvestite fetishizes clothing and women do not have fetishes. Current gender research tends to bear this out: despite the occasional fashion for women to wear masculine clothes, and despite the existence of

We can see this same model of temporary assertion of a female self whose very ephemeral nature enables the reassertion of masculine identity in the movement and the temporary transfer of authority within a transvestite narrative. The male author achieves, through a female narrator, participation in and control over a gendered voice that is simultaneously attractive and threatening. Like the real-world transvestite regarding his female image in the mirror, the transvestite narrator is both male and female or, in Defoe's and Richardson's terms, both writer and editor: one identity creates the other. As I will show, the male author plays out the rhetoric of gender in the metaphorical body of the text by enacting the structure of transvestism in narrative.

My analysis of two eighteenth-century novels, Defoe's *Roxana* and Richardson's *Clarissa,* clearly owes a great deal to the analytic structures of psychoanalytic theory. To some extent this use of psychoanalytic theory involves imposing an anachronistic structure and its concomitant values upon eighteenth-century texts. While one aim of the critic, however, is to recover the conventions of interpretation of the period, all approaches to the literature of the past are to some extent anachronistic, and this historical excavation is necessarily informed by one's theoretical assumptions. I have found the vocabulary of psychoanalysis particularly useful for recovering eighteenth-century England's gender expectations. Moreover, while the terminology may be anachronistic, the concern with the instability of categories and in particular the instability of categories of gender is emphatically not.

Indeed, Sarah Fielding, the sister of Henry Fielding and a close friend of Samuel Richardson, couched her elaborate *Remarks on Clarissa* in terms of a debate over Clarissa's womanliness and Lovelace's manliness. Her remarks take the form of a di-

---

women who dress and live all their lives as men, there seem to be no female equivalents of the men who *temporarily and periodically* dress as women for the gratification of their libidinal urges. For a brief discussion of novels written by women using a first-person male persona, see the Introduction.

alogue in which the two main characters, Bellario and Miss Gibson, argue Bellario's point that Clarissa has, by her unfeminine behavior, brought on her own tragic fate. Bellario says:

> Clarissa could not justly be accused of any material Fault, but that of wanting Affection for her Lover; for that he [Bellario] was sure, a Woman whose Mind was incapable of Love, could not be amiable, nor have any of those gentle Qualities which chiefly adorn the female Character.[26]

From this position Bellario—like the rake Belford in the novel, after whom he is clearly modeled—is gradually converted to Clarissa's cause. When he finally reverses his position, he explains his reversal by referring to his new analysis of Lovelace's character, thus defining the content of gender's categories by simple opposition. Clarissa's womanliness is definitively proven for Bellario by Lovelace's lack of manliness.

> Yes, replied Bellario, I am convinced [that Clarissa was capable of the strongest affection], and am surprised that I did not before see how much Lovelace's base unmanly Behavior justifies her in this point. (29)

Miss Gibson, who seems to be voicing Sarah Fielding's opinions in the dialogue, finally concludes that the "grand Moral" of the novel is that of "a Man's giving up every thing that is valuable, only because every thing that is valuable is in his power. Lovelace, . . . like one following an Ignis Fatuus through By-Paths and crooked Roads, . . . lost himself in the Eagerness of his own Pursuit" (54). This telling description is equally a description of the fate of any reader of *Clarissa* who is searching, as were both Lovelace and Clarissa, for absolutes of gender or of authority. As I show in later chapters, Richardson used the structure of narrative transvestism to engage his readers in this same search. And although his stated goal was the reaffirmation

---

[26]Sarah Fielding, *Remarks on Clarissa* ([1749] Los Angeles: University of California Press, 1985), p. 15. Further page numbers are in parentheses in the text.

of gendered categories, his novel so complicates those categories that Lovelace and Clarissa emerge as aspects of one character, each owing his or her continued life or power to the other.

The Construction and Transgression of Gender's Boundaries in Eighteenth-Century England

I have used scholary work from several fields in my effort to uncover the period's attempts to codify definitions of male and female sexuality and to set rules for the proper behavior of the genders in society. These include studies in the history of sexuality and medicine, sociology, and studies of conduct books and literary forms.[27] All these have shown me that we can find evidence of efforts to redefine sex and gender roles in every part of English society in the eighteenth century. The medical community was fascinated by hermaphrodites and by the challenge they posed to the concept of an absolute division between male and female genitalia.[28] Ministers, educators, and concerned parents produced a plethora of conduct books that delineated for young men and women the manners and even thoughts they must acquire to be either true men or true women.[29] Michel

[27]For a complete listing of the various works I have consulted other than those cited in the following notes, see the bibliography. In particular, see Laqueur for the history of medicine; Bloch, Boucé, Caplan, and Foucault for the history of sexuality; Armstrong and Poovey for domestic conduct books; Castle, *Masquerade and Civilization*, for an analysis of the deliberate confusion of gender at masquerades; and the essays in Miller, ed., *The Poetics of Gender*, and Rousseau and Porter, eds., *Sexual Underworlds of the Enlightenment*, for a variety of approaches.

[28]For details on hermaphrodites and on medical investigations of the biological differences between the sexes, see Stephen Greenblatt, "Fiction and Friction," in *Reconstructing Individualism: Autonomy, Individuality, and the Self in Western Thought*, ed. Thomas C. Heller, Morton Sosna, and David E. Wellbery (Stanford: Stanford University Press, 1986), pp. 30–52; Thomas Laqueur, "Orgasm, Generation, and the Politics of Reproductive Biology," *Representations* 14 (Spring 1986): 1–41; and several of the articles in Rousseau and Porter, eds., *Sexual Underworlds*.

[29]On the conduct books of the period, see Nancy Armstrong, *Desire and Domestic Fiction*; Mary Poovey, *The Proper Lady and the Woman Writer: Ideology as Style in the Works of Mary Wollstonecraft, Mary Shelley, and Jane Austen* (Chicago: University of Chicago Press, 1984); and Lawrence Stone, *The Family, Sex, and Marriage in England, 1500–1800* (New York: Harper and Row, 1977).

Foucault, of course, situates the rise of a sublimating discourse about sexuality in the eighteenth century, but at least in the first half of the century that discourse was not a substitute for experimentation and transgression so much as a commentary upon it.[30] In short, it is no accident that Virginia Woolf's Orlando changes sex in the eighteenth century so that s/he can escape the corruption of politics in Constantinople, where s/he has been an ambassador, and instead experience society's other, feminine realm.[31] Of course part of Woolf's project in her novel is to redefine those masculine and feminine realms, but this redefinition, too, is appropriate to the century in which Orlando was transformed. In eighteenth-century England, almost all matters pertaining to gendered behavior were up for discussion.

Two historians with very different theoretical and methodological approaches, Christopher Hill and Lawrence Stone, both detail the social and political upheaval that found much of its expression in the experimental transgression of traditional boundaries between the genders.[32] Hill is, of course, primarily concerned with the political instability of the seventeenth century, but he makes the case that his ranters and levelers went underground, as it were, from the political arena to the domestic one. The world that continued to be turned upside down was that of traditional moral codes—particularly those pertaining

[30]Foucault, *The History of Sexuality*, pp. 23–24: "Toward the beginning of the eighteenth century, there emerged a political, economic, and technical incitement to talk about sex. And not so much in the form of a general theory of sexuality as in the form of analysis, stocktaking, classification, and specification, of quantitative or causal studies. . . . Between the state and the individual, sex became an issue, and a public issue no less; a whole web of discourses, knowledges, analyses, and injunctions settled upon it."

[31]Virginia Woolf, *Orlando* (New York: Harcourt Brace, 1928), p. 137. See also p. 139: "The change seemed to have been accomplished painlessly and completely and in such a way that Orlando herself showed no surprise at it. Many people, taking this into account, and holding that such a change of sex is against nature, have been at great pains to prove (1) that Orlando had always been a woman, (2) that Orlando is at this moment a man. Let biologists and psychologists determine. It is enough for us to state the simple fact; Orlando was a man till the age of thirty; when he became a woman and has remained so ever since."

[32]Christopher Hill, *The World Turned Upside Down: Radical Ideas during the English Revolution* (New York: Penguin, 1972), and Stone, *Family, Sex, and Marriage*.

to sexual behavior—and of power relations between men and women within the family.

> The sexual revolution which was an important part of the introduction of the protestant ethic meant replacing property marriage (with love outside marriage) by a monogamous partnership, ostensibly based on mutual love, and a business partnership in the affairs of the family. The wife was subordinate to her husband, but no slave. The abolition of monasteries and nunneries symbolized the replacement of the celibate ideal ("stinking chastity" as Bale called it) by the concept of chastity in marriage. The dual standard of sexual conduct was replaced, at least as an ideal, by a single standard applied to both sexes.[33]

Hill goes on to detail the continuing revolutionary exchange between changes in domestic life and political and religious upheaval. He pays particular attention to the crux at which the political and legal system intersects with domestic relations: marriage laws and customs.

Lawrence Stone, who makes the focus of his investigation explicit in the title of his *The Family, Sex, and Marriage in England*, argues that a new concept of the individual is promulgated in the eighteenth century, and that the crucible in which that individual was formed was the period's rapidly changing conceptions of what makes a man, what makes a woman, and how the two should relate to each other. Stone provides a complement to Hill's political discussion with his exploration of what he calls "affective individualism"[34] and its expression in a new emphasis on domesticity, romantic love, and the companionate marriage.

Although Stone generally sees eighteenth-century society becoming increasingly stable as the newly unique and self-absorbed individual finds an affective home in the nuclear fam-

[33]Hill, *World Turned Upside Down*, p. 306. Chap. 15, "Base Impudent Kisses," is particularly concerned with the revolution in sexual standards and morality.

[34]He defines "affective individualism" as "a change in how the individual regarded himself in relation to society (the growth of individualism) and how he behaved and felt towards other human beings, particularly his wife and children on the one hand, and parents and kin on the other (the growth of affect)" (150).

ily, he documents ample confusion, fear, and disruption along the way. In particular, his chapters on sexual behavior and his many citations from contemporary conduct books show that the individual's pursuit of happiness and his pursuit of it through sexual expression had made a great rent in the social fabric which had previously helped to hold the individual within an established and gendered code of behavior.[35]

Toward the end of his book, Stone notes that "the three most common subjects in the advertisement columns of eighteenth-century periodicals were cures for venereal disease, cosmetics and books—in that order."[36] One could hardly invent a more evocative list for individuals in search of a new discourse within which to define themselves. Each item seems to promise some code of relations to others and some instruction for the self. The public offering of cures for venereal disease not only acknowledges the sexual activity that makes such cures necessary but it also promises that the consequences of such sexual activity are not irrevocable.[37] Cosmetics, and the conventions for applying them, provide a mask of approved masculine or feminine beauty. And books of any kind offer a private experience of intimate connection with an other—whether it is with the author or the fictional characters.

Together these items echo eighteenth-century England's newly impassioned questioning of categories—both sexual and other. The sexual license that is undoubtedly a feature of every age meshed in eighteenth-century England with an explosion of new discourse about the absolute nature of categories in general and in particular of the categories of behavior by which men and women defined themselves.

[35]"Freedom of sexual expression was one of the many by-products of the eighteenth-century pursuit of happiness." Stone, *Family, Sex, and Marriage*, p. 328.

[36]Ibid., p. 379.

[37]James Boswell, whose many cases of venereal disease did nothing to diminish his obsessive sexual activity, took this promise to heart. See Boswell, *London Journal* (New York: McGraw Hill, 1980), and William Ober, "Boswell's Clap," *Boswell's Clap and Other Essays: Medical Analyses of Literary Men's Afflictions* (Carbondale: Southern Illinois University Press, 1979), pp. 1–42.

This new discourse eventually found its literary form in the novel, as Ruth Perry says:

The challenges in English society of the later seventeenth century and the early eighteenth century redefined the ways in which women were to function within that society, and at the same time prepared the context for the novel. Inasmuch as novels chart the private voyages of individual minds, these tracings were not a possible subject matter for popular fiction until the Reformation had emphasized the separate struggle and salvation of each single person; until the entrepreneurial spirit of capitalism had replaced community ties with sentimental attachment to individualism; until city living provided the anonymity which made private experience interesting to others; until people were reading and writing enough so that these private acts of consciousness were a substantial part of life for a sizable proportion of the population.[38]

But, as Thomas Laqueur says, the struggle over the old hierarchical model of categories also took more material forms.

Writers from the eighteenth century onward sought in the facts of biology a justification for cultural and political differences between the sexes that were crucial to the articulation of both feminist and antifeminist arguments. . . . Thus, women's bodies in their corporeal, scientifically accessible concreteness, in the very nature of their bones, nerves, and, most important, reproductive organs came to bear an enormous new weight of cultural meaning in the Enlightenment. Arguments about the very existence of female sexual passion, about women's special capacity to control what desires they did have, and about their moral nature generally were all part of a new enterprise seeking to discover the anatomical and physiological characteristics that distinguished men from women. As the natural body itself became the gold standard of social discourse, the bodies of women became the battleground for redefining the most ancient, the most intimate, the most fundamental of human relations: that of women to man.[39]

Cross-dressing neatly combines these efforts to discover just what differentiated women from men with these "private acts of

38Ruth Perry, *Women, Letters, and the Novel* (New York: AMS Press, 1980), pp. ix–x.
39Laqueur, "Orgasm, Generation, and the Politics of Reproductive Biology," p. 18.

consciousness" by which individuals come to define themselves. And the ambivalent social response to public cross-dressing reveals its power; it was threatening precisely because it was appealing.

To start with the most obvious example, cross-dressing was common enough to be a comedy staple and yet challenging enough to be a source of considerable outrage. Men had for centuries played women on the stage, but now women also played men, and perhaps as a consequence men feared that what was meant as play might have disastrous consequences.

This fear is clearly expressed in the anti-theatricality tracts of the seventeenth century, which fulminated against the adultera-tion of the male gender by male actors who wore women's clothing on the stage. One of the supposed dangers of such theatrical cross-dressing was that the male actor might degener-ate into a woman. This reportedly happened to a warrior who, taking off his masquerade, found a woman beneath his clothes. Laura Levine comments astutely upon this apocryphal story: "There is nothing essential about this 'valiant man's' identity: it slips away from him with his clothes. At the same time there is something permanent and, therefore, essential and clearly mon-strous locked away 'inside' him, his capacity—envisioned al-most as a bodily structure—for womanishness itself."[40]

Thomas Laqueur cites a tale of a young girl who by vigorous exertion "ruptured the ligaments by which [the male genitalia] had been enclosed" and so at the age of fifteen became a man. He further notes:

> Seventeenth-century audiences still gave credence to a whole col-lection of tales, going back at least to Pliny, that illustrate the structural similarities and thus the mutability of male and female bodies. Sir Thomas Browne, in his *Enquiries into Vulgar and Com-mon Errors* (1646), devotes an entire chapter to the question of whether "every hare is both male and female." He concludes that

[40]Laura Levine, "Men in Women's Clothing: Antitheatricality and Effeminization from 1579–1642," *Criticism* 28 (Spring 1986): 135.

"as for the mutation of sexes, or transition of one into another, we cannot deny it in Hares, in being observable in Man."

However, some theorists declared that only the more primitive bodies of women were subject to these alarming mutations: "We therefore never find in any true story that any man ever became a woman, because Nature tends always toward what is most perfect and not, on the contrary, to perform in such a way that what is perfect should become imperfect."[41]

The problem was double edged: men masquerading as women might find themselves trapped in the devalued realm of the feminine; and women, by masquerading as men, might usurp male power and prerogatives—not least of which was the right to masquerade (without lasting consequences) as women.

By the eighteenth century, men who masqueraded as women on the stage still provoked anxiety, but now the expression of that anxiety was more likely to be laughter than outrage. In the long run of *The Beggar's Opera*, for example, performances of this already transgressive satire were often enlivened by having a male actor play the part of sweet, innocent Polly. Patricia Spacks cites a death notice from the *Gentleman's Magazine* "of one Mrs. Fitzherbert, who died of hysterics, having begun to laugh uncontrollably at seeing Polly represented by a man."[42] Dying of hysterics is, of course, not quite dying of laughter. It bespeaks an element of shock, perhaps even panic, at this transgression made material.[43] In the course of the play, Polly is revealed as not

[41]Laqueur, "Orgasm, Generation, and the Politics of Reproductive Biology," pp. 13–14.

[42]Patricia Meyer Spacks, *John Gay* (New York: Twayne, 1965), p. 127.

[43]In "Fiction and Friction," Stephen Greenblatt detects an intimate link between the renaissance tradition of cross-dressing on the stage and the self-fashioning in which the drama was engaged. "Shakespearean comedy constantly appeals to the body, in particular to sexuality, as the heart of its theatrical magic; 'great creating nature,' the principle by which the world is and must be peopled, is the comic playwright's tutelary spirit. . . . These [cross-dressed] figures function as modes of translation between distinct social discourses, channels through which cultural power is circulated" (46). "Why should that fashioning be bound up with cross-dressing? . . . In part, I suggest, because the transformation of gender identity

so sweet and innocent after all, which only makes more apt the seeming incongruity of a male actor in the role.

We'll never know whether Mrs. Fitzherbert died of delight or terror, but it is easy to see that both men and women feared that the actresses who began to play male roles on the stage in this period might also take on the trappings of male power in the real world. Charlotte Charke (the poet laureate Colley Cibber's daughter) brought that fear to life when she took advantage of her great success at playing male roles in the theater to continue playing male roles off stage. Charke had dressed in men's clothes to make her way about town more easily. She even claimed to have once masqueraded as a highwayman to rob her father's coach, a claim that provides us with a wonderful allegory for her theft of his male prerogative. And for a time she lived as a married "man," a Mr. Brown, and took a Mrs. Brown as her wife.[44]

The lesbian marriage that Charlotte Charke played at while masquerading as a man was lived out by the famous Ladies of Llangollen (Eleanor Butler and Sarah Ponsonby), who later in the century overcame the scandal of their union to become an example of the ideal companionate marriage, championed and sentimentalized by writers from Sheridan to Wordsworth.[45]

---

figures the emergence of an individual out of a twinned sexual nature. . . . Separation from the female, the crux of male individuation, is inverted in the rites of cross-dressing; such characters as Rosalind and Viola pass through the state of being men in order to become women. Shakespearean women are in this sense the representation of Shakespearean men, the projected mirror images of masculine self-differentiation. I should add that in the tragedies these mirror images become nightmares, and self-differentiation gives way to dreams of self-slaughter" (50–52).

[44]For a fuller account of Charke's life, see her *A Narrative of the Life of Mrs. Charlotte Charke (Youngest Daughter of Colley Cibber, Esq.), Written by Herself*, ed. Leonard R. N. Ansley (Gainesville, Fla.: Scholarly Facsimiles & Reprints, 1969). See also Patricia Meyer Spacks, *Imagining a Self: Autobiography and the Novel in Eighteenth-Century England* (Cambridge: Harvard University Press, 1976), and Sidonie Smith, *A Poetics of Women's Autobiography: Marginality and the Fictions of Self-Representation* (Bloomington: Indiana University Press, 1987), chap. 6, "A Narrative of the Life of Mrs. Charlotte Charke," pp. 102–22).

[45]For details about the Ladies of Llangollen, see Lillian Faderman, *Surpassing the Love of Men: Romantic Friendship and Love between Women from the Renaissance to the Present* (New York: William Morrow, 1981), and Elizabeth Mavor, ed., *A Year with the Ladies of Llangollen* (New York: Penguin, 1986).

Less palatable to society, although a boon to certain forms of broadside literature, were those women who disguised themselves as men to gain freedom of movement and of employment in a society that rigidly limited women's lives to the domestic sphere. In particular, women who served in the army and navy were a challenge to the perceived weakness and timorousness of the one sex and an affront to the supposed natural strength and courage of the other. In a very few cases such women, when discovered, were awarded honorable discharges and military pensions, but for the most part women who lived as men were taking extraordinary risks.[46]

Henry Fielding details those risks along with the sexual perversion that was assumed to accompany such cross-dressing in *The Female Husband*. The tone of this little pamphlet is most remarkable for its outrage against the violation of sexual and social categories. While remaining titillatingly vague about the physical details (we never quite know, for example, why Mary/

[46]For the histories of women passing as men, see John Ashton, *Eighteenth Century Waifs* ([1887] Freeport, N.Y.: Books for Libraries Press, 1972); Derek Jarret, *England in the Age of Hogarth* (New York: Viking, 1974); and J. R. Western, *The English Militia in the Eighteenth Century* (London: Routledge and Kegan Paul, 1965). Famous cases include Mrs. Christina Davis, who joined the army in hopes of meeting a husband. She enlisted under the name of Christopher Welch and was sued for paternity over the illegitimate child of a woman whose advances she had spurned (Ashton, 179). She was finally discovered while she was unconscious from a wound. Mary Anne Talbot was another famous soldier and sailor and was reputed to have been forced into transvestism on board ship by a Captain Bowen. The story of Hannah Snell, who, as Jemmy Gray, was stripped for flogging without her sex being discovered (Ashton, p. 186), is typically improbable in its physical details. For even more intriguing vagueness in the physical and sexual realm, see Henry Fielding, *The Female Husband* (London, 1746), reprinted in *The Female Husband and Other Writings*, ed. Claude E. Jones, (28–51) (Liverpool: Liverpool University Press, 1960).

On the risks that transvestites took, see Ackroyd, *Dressing Up*. "Transvestism was repressed; the punishments for those who engaged in it were often harsh—the penalty in England was to be placed in the stocks or dragged through the streets in an open cart and in France, as late as 1760, transvestites could be burned to death" (57). Ackroyd's book also includes accounts of many famous transvestites, including Moll Cutpurse, the Abbé de Choisy, Christina Davies, Hannah Snell, Mary Anne Talbot, and Anne Boddy and Mary Read, the "female pirates."

On the challenge to the division between public and private inherent in female cross-dressing, see Lynn Friedli, " 'Passing women'—A Study of Gender Boundaries in the Eighteenth Century," in Rousseau and Porter, eds., *Sexual Underworlds*, pp. 234–60.

George's many wives failed to discover that she was not a he, and why they all professed to have been sexually satisfied by her male organ), Fielding is clear about the threat that Mary/George posed to the proper social and gender hierarchy.[47]

Fielding's subtitle states that Mary/George's story was "Taken from Her own Mouth since her Confinement." He thus uses narrative to reconfine this woman who has overstepped the limitations of her sex by asserting her freedom, independence, and what seems to be a rampant female sexuality. She has, more disturbingly, so clothed her female body in artifice that she has become an extremely successful male. Fielding's descriptions of "his" popularity as a husband raise the question of whether Mary's male costume has actually made her into a man or perhaps into something even better than a man. Fielding's account of Mary/George's adventures leads him to some contradictory statements about the unnatural acts to which our natural human appetites can lead:

> But if once our carnal appetites are let loose, without those prudent and secure guides, there is no excess and disorder which they are not liable to commit, even while they pursue their natural satisfaction; and, which may seem still more strange, there is nothing monstrous and unnatural, which they are not capable of inventing, nothing so brutal and shocking which they have not actually committed. (29)

In his mock heroic tale Fielding at once exploits and decries the conflation of sexual categories (and all that depends upon them) by which Mary/George created herself. In referring to her, for example, he freely mixes male and female pronouns within the

---

[47]Henry Fielding, *The Female Husband*. For an excellent reading of this pamphlet, see Terry Castle, "Matters Not Fit to Be Mentioned," pp. 602–22. Castle reads the piece as an "allegory of transgression" (607) and makes the case that Fielding's own ambivalence about Mary/George is enacted in his use of the mock heroic which "grants power to its target at the same time that it tries to minimize it" (612). This is, of course, one of the characteristics of satire—it immortalizes what it sets out to destroy—but in this case this boomerang effect is complicated by the layers of sexual and narrative ambiguity.

same sentence. That confusing but liberating conflation of sexual categories is exploited to its fullest by the Chevalier d'Éon later in the century.

D'Éon was a diplomat and spy for the court of Louis XV who, after being much decorated as a military guard, first made himself valuable to the king by insinuating himself as a woman into the Russian court. Later, as a French diplomat in England he claimed that he was in fact a woman who had always been masquerading as a man, and he settled down to live as a woman in London. After the French court pensioned him off to rid themselves of the embarrassment of speculation about his sex and of vexing questions about the location of certain highly sensitive documents (whose nature and ultimate disposition remain fittingly obscure), d'Éon (now calling himself "the chevalière") made money by competing in fencing exhibitions while dressed as a woman. In his later years the frenzy of betting on his biological sex had reached such proportions that "*The Morning Post* declared two hundred thousand pounds to be at stake."[48]

The Chevalier's contradictory claims about which was his true self and which the masquerade emphasize the permeability of the boundaries between gender categories and the fact that manliness and womanliness are not absolute qualities but relative terms. It is easy to see that such a chameleon-like identity afforded him a kind of protective coloration in his role as a spy (or perhaps double agent) for the French court, but it is, of course, impossible to say whether the spy created the chameleon of gender, or the fluid identity created the spy. In any case, the Chevalier d'Éon's story exemplifies the process that is the very essence of transvestism.

As they are to the spy—especially to the double agent—spe-

---

[48]Friedli, " 'Passing women,' " p. 245. For biographies of the Chevalier d'Éon, see Cynthia Cox, *The Enigma of the Age: The Strange Story of the Chevalier d'Éon* (London: Longman's, 1966); Frederick Gaillardet, *The Memoirs of the Chevalier d'Éon*, trans. Antonia White (London: Anthony Blond, 1970); and Edna Nixon, *Royal Spy: The Strange Case of the Chevalier d'Éon* (New York: Reynal, 1965).

cifics and biographical details are death to the transvestite; he cannot function unless his true identity is vaguely blurred. The Chevalier managed to make a career out of his temporary projection of himself into various other selves and, toward the end of his life, rather successfully exploited even the scandal that greeted each switch.

The same elements of scandal, of sexual license, of the possibility of revealing a truer self through disguise, and of the muddying of all boundaries that we see in these stories of famous eighteenth-century transvestites were also present in the more socially sanctioned transvestism that was such a feature of the period's popular masquerades. Terry Castle details the frequent adoption of transvestite costume at these masquerades and the sexual license that accompanied such a "stylised assault on gender boundaries":

> Transvestite costume was perhaps the most common offence against decorum. Women strutted in jack-boots and breeches, while men primped in furbelows and flounces. Horace Walpole described passing "for a good mask" as an old woman at a masquerade in 1742. Other male masqueraders disguised themselves as witches, bawds, nursery-maids and shepherdesses. . . . The anti-masquerade writers, not surprisingly, found cross-dressing a palpable sign of masquerade depravity. The author of the *Short Remarks* complained that the confounding of garments had ever "been used by Wantons, to savour their lascivious Designs."[49]

[49]Castle, "The Culture of Travesty: Sexuality and Masquerade in Eighteenth-Century England," in Rousseau and Porter, eds., *Sexual Underworlds*, p. 163. For a more thorough investigation of masquerade and its meanings, see Terry Castle, *Masquerade and Civilization*. In this book she very nicely captures the resonance carried by the seemingly simple act of cross-dressing: "One might begin, at a slant, with the ancient analogy between clothing and language. The eighteenth century perceived a deep correspondence between the two: not only was language the 'dress' of thought—that lucid covering in which the mind decorously clothed its ideas—but clothing was in turn a kind of discourse. Then, as now, dress spoke symbolically of the human being beneath its folds. It reinscribed a person's sex, rank, age, occupation—all the distinctive features of the self. Modern semiotics has confirmed the force of the analogy: like language, clothing is after all a system of signs, and a means of symbolic communication. Like speech acts, different costumes carry conventional meanings; clothing opens itself everywhere to interpretation by others, in accordance with prevailing systems of sartorial inscriptions. Clothing inescapably serves a signifying function within culture; it is in fact an institution inseparable from culture" (55).

Castle goes on to note that transvestism posed a threat to more than conventional definitions of gender and sexuality:

> Whether practised in assembly-rooms, theaters, brothels, public gardens, or at the masquerade itself (which flourished in London from the 1720s on), collective sartorial transformation offered a cathartic escape from the self and a suggestive revision of ordinary experience. . . . Yet travesty had an even more subversive function in eighteenth-century life. It posed an intimate challenge to the ordering patterns of culture itself.[50]

Questions about the truths of masks as opposed to the truths of the unmasked naturally lead to questions about the stability of all categories. The natural might become the unnatural, male might become female. These challenges were carried further in a more abstract realm later in the century by those "bluestocking" women who clothed themselves in male education and rhetoric and who thereby posed a real threat to the established order of power and gender. Angeline Goreau points out that:

> The phrase "the feminine sphere" comes up repeatedly in letters, diaries, etiquette manuals, and other contemporary texts; it is used synonymously with the "private domain" or "the home," while the male province delineates "the world." Any foray into what was seen as male preserve, whether real or imagined, verbal or actual, was seen as a negation of femininity.[51]

Horace Walpole carried this attack on transgressive women one step further by declaring that Mary Wollstonecraft's transgressions into the male intellectual domain negated even her humanity. He called her a "hyena in petticoats." Even Mary Astell, who as a devout Christian was a firm believer in a divinely ordained hierarchy, was not pleased to find her writings praised as being above a woman's capabilities

> since the Men being the Historians, they seldom condescend to record the great and good Actions of Women; and when they take

[50]Castle, "The Culture of Travesty," p. 157.
[51]Angeline Goreau, "Two English Women in the Seventeenth Century: Notes for an Anatomy of Feminine Desire," in Ariès and Béjin, eds., Western Sexuality, p. 106.

notice of them, 'tis with this wise Remark, That such Women *acted above their Sex*. By which one must suppose that they wou'd have their Readers understand, That they were not Women who did those Great Actions, but that they were Men in Petticoats![52]

The bluestockings who adopted male education and rhetoric gained access to greater intellectual freedom, just as those women who passed as men in the army gained greater physical freedom. The rhetorical "dressing down" of narrative transvestism gave men access to the same female realm that women were trying to escape. What was imprisoning to a woman was liberating for a man because his participation in that female realm was temporary and because she functioned as a defining other for his male self. As Simone de Beauvoir points out in *The Second Sex:* "Man seeks in woman the Other as Nature and as his fellow being. . . . [S]he is the source of his being and the realm that he subjugates to his will; Nature is a vein of gross materiality in which the soul is imprisoned, and she is the supreme reality."[53]

[52]Mary Astell, letter to Elizabeth Elstob in 1705, quoted in Ruth Perry, *The Celebrated Mary Astell: An Early English Feminist* (Chicago: University of Chicago Press, 1986), p. 25. On the subject of Astell's "masculine" mind, see Perry, p. 79: "Norris, as I have said, was so astonished at the philosophical abilities of his interlocutor that he assumed his equally surprised readers would be tempted to question whether my Correspondent be really a Woman or no." Perry also quotes Francis Atterbury on p. 219: "I take 'em to be of an extraordinary Nature, considering that they came from the Pen of a Woman. Indeed one would not imagine that a Woman had written 'em. There is not an expression that carries the least Air of her Sex from the Beginning to the End of it."
Of course some women were so thoroughly assimilated to the traditional hierarchy and its judgment of women that they essentially identified with their oppressors. Susan Groag Bell and Karen M. Offen, in *Women, the Family, and Freedom: The Debate in Documents*, vol. 1, *1750–1880* (Stanford: Stanford University Press, 1983), record Hannah More's response to Wollstonecraft's *Vindication of the Rights of Women:* "Only one year after the appearance of Wollstonecraft's *Vindication*, More wrote to a male friend: 'I have been much pestered to read the "rights of Women," but am invincibly resolved not to do it. Of all jargon I hate metaphysical jargon; besides there is something fantastic and absurd in the very title. How many ways there are of being ridiculous! I am sure I have as much liberty as I can make good use of, now I am an old maid [she was forty-eight], and when I was a young one, I had, I dare say, more than was good for me" (84).
[53]Simone de Beauvoir, *The Second Sex*, ed. and trans. H. M. Parshley ([1952] New York: Vintage Books, 1974), p. 162.

It is not by accident that in this period in which women were seeking power and mobility in the real world through male dress, men sought power in the imaginative world through an ersatz female voice. Narrative transvestism offered to the eighteenth-century male writer a structure that allowed him to explore his society's experimental transgression of boundaries even while it afforded him some distance from and control over the risks he was taking. By "becoming" a woman, the male writer could temporarily assume the power of generation—of corporeal existence and creation—while simultaneously extending his power over women from the social or real realm to the imaginative one. That imaginative power then redounded to the real world; male writers controlled the voices and fates of their female characters, and their female readers found in novels an articulate woman on whom they might model themselves but who had, in fact, been invented by a man.

These cultural disturbances, expressed in terms of gender, were also generic disturbances. For example, the fifty years before Richardson are the heyday of satire, which defines itself as a "pudding," an antigeneric genre. The novel, and in particular narrative transvestism in the novel, offered one way to turn such generic chaos and the accompanying sense of loss into a new kind of structure: one that embraces the disorder of process and accomplishes its form over time. As a suggestive transgression of the rhetorical and imaginative equivalents of gender's social boundaries, narrative transvestism allows us to see that an asymmetrical sex and gender system gives rise to its own rhetoric of identity and difference, and this rhetoric gains expression in literary structures as well as other social practices.

Transvestism and Eighteenth-Century English Literature

Literary criticism has traditionally viewed eighteenth-century literature as a study in contrasts. We divide it into the opposite poles of the Augustans, with their emphasis on the role of the writer in society, and the Romantics, who were in search of a personal and individual revelation. Or we contrast the satirists, who were intent on reforming political and literary hierarchies, with the inward-turning mad poets of the midcentury, or the detailed realism of Defoe and Fielding with the phantasm of the Gothic. And within those divisions we further divide the center from the margin. In the center we have the canonical representatives of the period's literature: Swift, Pope, and the Scriblerians; Johnson, Boswell, and the literary club; Wordsworth and Coleridge, and, just barely making it into the century, Jane Austen. The margin is all that the center defines as other: poets like Colley Cibber, whose concerns were foolish ones; the first novelists, who abandoned the traditional literary forms; and women, from whom any writing was an affront to established social categories.

These careful divisions of satirist from Romantic and center from margin reflect the period's own passion for reason, categories, and symmetrical structure. In reaction to the political, religious, and social upheaval of the seventeenth century, many eighteenth-century writers, scientists, and philosophers clung to the traditional Western epistemology, which ordered the world by dividing it into opposite poles. This binary view of the world goes back at least as far as Plato, who was at such pains to distinguish the mere body from the immortal soul and for whom women were limited to bodily existence while men might transcend their mortality in philosophy.[54]

Such a dualistic view lends itself to a method of definition by

[54]For example, Elizabeth V. Spelman, in "Woman as Body: Ancient and Contemporary Views," *Feminist Studies* 8 (Spring 1982): pp. 111–15, claims that Plato defines women in terms of their bodies and men in terms of their souls, and that women are continually used as negative examples to philosophers. She summarizes Plato's distinction between men and women: "The body, with its deceptive senses, keeps us from real knowledge. . . . All that bodies in unison can create are more bodies—the children women bear—which are mortal, subject to change and decay. But souls in unison can create 'something lovelier and less mortal than human seed.' . . . Unless a man lives righteously now, he will as his next incarnation 'pass into a woman.' "

Unlike Spelman, Genevieve Lloyd claims in *The Man of Reason, "Male" and "Female" in Western Philosophy* (London: Methuen, 1984) that "mind's domination of mat-

opposition: the I versus the not-I; the self against the other. And the fundamental social expression of this binary structure is the perceived opposition of the genders: man is man by virtue of not being woman. Woman is all that man fears and abhors.

The great advantage of a worldview that situates the two genders at opposite poles is that the boundary between the two is (at least temporarily) very distinct. And for the pole doing the defining, this boundary becomes the basis of a hierarchy of power.[55]

The great disadvantage (for that hierarchy of power) is that the two poles are inextricably linked; each pole is defined only by its opposition to the other. Thus the male must continually redefine the female to assert his identity as not-female. Moreover, the polarized structure continually undermines itself: the male who is defining himself as not-female, or the self who exists because he is not-other, turns out to be deeply dependent upon this opposite to which he denies all connection. Thus the defining self can never simply exist. He must continually reaffirm his selfhood by negating all others whose very existence threatens his identity.[56]

---

ter . . . was not explicitly associated with the male-female distinction, but rather with the master-slave relation" (16). Nevertheless Lloyd also situates man's definition of woman as other and lesser at the heart of Western philosophy: "The maleness of the man of Reason . . . is no superficial linguistic bias" (ix). "What had to be shed in developing culturally prized rationality was, from the start, symbolically associated with femaleness. . . . These symbolic associations lingered in later refinements of the idea and the ideals of Reason; maleness remained associated with a clear, determinate mode of thought, femaleness with the vague and indeterminate. In the Pythagorean table of opposites, formulated in the sixth century BC, femaleness was explicitly linked with the unbounded—the vague, the indeterminate—as against the bounded—the precise and clearly determined. The Pythagoreans saw the world as a mixture of principles associated with determinate form, seen as good, and others associated with formlessness—the unlimited, irregular or disorderly—which were seen as bad or inferior. . . . "Male," like the other terms on its side of the table, was construed as superior to its opposite; and the basis for this superiority was its association with the primary Pythagorean contrast between form and formlessness" (3).

[55]On this link between the suppression of an other and hierarchies of power, see in particular Foucault, *The History of Sexuality*, and Peter Stallybrass and Allon White, *The Politics and Poetics of Transgression* (Ithaca: Cornell University Press, 1986).

[56]As part of a discussion of deconstructive criticism, which he characterizes as "the critical operation by which such oppositions can be partly undermined, or by which

Although much of eighteenth-century English thought was rooted in this dualistic worldview I have briefly described, the period was also intensely aware of the limitations of such a view and deeply anxious about the possibility of the structure collapsing in the face of social and political change. Particularly in the literature of the traditional canon, we find an awareness of the fragility of such a dualistic structure and an uncomfortable acknowledgment of that structure's dependence upon all that it denies.

A close look at each of our central literary figures reveals, for example, that they all dragged themselves into the center from some place on the margins of literature and society, and, more importantly, that they brought to the position the knowledge that it is, in fact, the margin that defines the center, and the boundary between the two is often disturbingly permeable.

The writer who is perhaps the most emblematic of our image of the eighteenth century is Alexander Pope, whose balanced couplets and compelling aphorisms demonstrate the elevated and somewhat detached perspective that we expect of the period. But Pope also lavished loving attention (in *The Dunciad* and other satires) upon the very filth and disorder he abhorred. And

---

they can be shown partly to undermine each other in the process of textual meaning," Terry Eagleton, in *Literary Theory*, nicely summarizes the anxious assertions of a man redefining himself as not-woman: "Woman is the opposite, the "other" of man: she is non-man, defective man, assigned a chiefly negative value in relation to the male first principle. But equally man is what he is only by virtue of ceaselessly shutting out this other or opposite, defining himself in antithesis to it, and his whole identity is therefore caught up and put at risk in the very gesture by which he seeks to assert his unique, autonomous existence. Woman is not just an other in the sense of something beyond his ken, but an other intimately related to him as the image of what he is not, and therefore as an essential reminder of what he is. Man therefore needs this other even as he spurns it, is constrained to give a positive identity to what he regards as no-thing. Not only is his own being parasitically dependent upon the woman, and upon the act of excluding and subordinating her, but one reason why such exclusion is necessary is because she may not be quite so other after all. Perhaps she stands as a sign of something in man himself which he needs to repress, expel beyond his own being, relegate to a securely alien region beyond his own definitive limits. Perhaps what is outside is also somehow inside, what is alien also intimate— so that man needs to police the absolute frontier between the two realms as vigilantly as he does just because it may always be transgressed, has always been transgressed already, and is much less absolute than it appears" (132–33).

in so doing he acknowledged (however ambivalently) that in the pairs of squalor and magnificence, deformity and beauty, bad poetry and good poetry, each term owes its existence to its opposite term.[57] The parceling out of value between the opposing terms is a risky activity. Values are unstable in a structure in which the poles can be switched or transposed while retaining their relative positions. The Dunces of the world, for example, prompted Pope to turn the dross of bad poetry into the miracle of *The Dunciad;* in so doing he risked either having his poetry polluted by the bad poems he sought to annihilate or immortalizing that bad poetry within his own.

In his "Epistle to Dr. Arbuthnot," Pope acknowledges that his own poetic gift is a similarly ambiguous thing:

> Why did I write? what sin to me unknown
> Dipt me in Ink, my Parents' or my own?
> As yet a Child, nor yet a Fool to Fame,
> I lispt in Numbers, for the Numbers came.
> I left no Calling for this idle trade,
> No Duty broke, no Father dis-obey'd
> The Muse but serv'd to ease some Friend, not Wife
> To help me thro' this long Disease, my Life.[58]

The measured rhythms, the careful rhymes of the poetry serve to contain the pain and disguise the vulnerability of a line such as "this long Disease, my Life," but what Pope is revealing here

[57]Stallybrass and White make much of this point in *Politics and Poetics of Transgression,* p. 105: "Precisely because the suppression and distancing of the physical body became the very sign of rationality, wit and judgment, the grotesque physical body existed as what Macherey calls a 'determining absent presence' in the classical body of Enlightenment poetic and critical discourse, a raging set of phantoms and concrete conditions to be forcefully rejected, projected or unacknowledged. Hence the apparent paradox that writers who were the great champions of a classical discursive body including Dryden, Swift and Pope spent so much time writing the grotesque, exorcising it, charging it to others, using and adopting its very terms whilst attempting to purify the language of the tribe. The production and reproduction of a body of classical writing required a labour of suppression, a perpetual work of exclusion upon the grotesque body."

[58]Alexander Pope, "An Epistle from Mr. Pope to Dr. Arbuthnot" (1735), in *Poetry and Prose of Alexander Pope,* ed. Aubrey Williams (Boston: Houghton Mifflin, 1969), lines 125–32.

is that the Olympian perspective of, for example, the *Essay on Man* was achieved at great cost. The gift (lisping in numbers) that allows him to write the "Epistles to Several Persons" is also the source of the pain that prompts him to write. The muse is both the cause of and the comfort in "this long Disease, my Life," and keeping the disease separate from the art is a lifelong balancing act.

Pope's revelation is another aspect of the dilemma posed by a binary structure in which the self is defined against all that it is not: the opposing poles can never be far enough apart. They are always in danger of becoming transposed. The great open secret of the eighteenth century is this: the inhabitants of the Enlightenment were afraid of the dark, and the man of reason feared that he might go mad.

In the midst of their fear, some eighteenth-century authors set out to shore up their shaky hierarchy of values, and others chose to exploit the instability of that hierarchy. Samuel Johnson, who did in fact fear that he would go mad,[59] gives us an emblem for both these responses in his *Life of Pope*. Even as he participates in literature's enduring effort to transform madness into reason and chaos into order, Johnson recoils from Pope's playful transformation of relative values. In a brief passage that is almost an aside, he pays homage to Pope's effort at alchemy while reminding us that the luster of Pope's poetic imagery is ephemeral— that the poet, like the alchemist, always returns to the lead that defines him.

Johnson is writing about Pope's famous grotto—the elaborate aesthetic hideaway that he'd built under the London road on his estate, Twickenham—and he makes this simultaneously astute and arch pronouncement: "As some men try to be proud of their defects, he extracted an ornament from an inconvenience [that of having to go under the London road] and vanity produced a grotto where necessity enforced a passage."[60]

---

[59]James Boswell documents these fears in his *Life of Samuel Johnson* (Garden City, N.Y.: Doubleday, 1946).

[60]Samuel Johnson, "Life of Pope," in *The Lives of the English Poets*, ed. George Birbeck Hill (Oxford: Clarendon Press, 1935), 3:135.

Johnson's sentence contains in microcosm several aspects of his era's deep and explicit concern with categories and with the transvaluation of those categories through art. In a very short span of prose he presents us with several shifts in the relative values of pride and defects, ornament and inconvenience, and vanity and necessity so that it becomes hard to know how to draw the boundaries between these supposed opposites.

In this shifting hierarchy of values, art and artifice are at times indistinguishable, and the noble artistic effort to escape the constraints of mere mortality reveals its roots in a foolish claim to immortality. "As some men try to be proud of their defects," Pope refused to be limited by an inconvenience; he transformed it into an ornament. Thus Pope's vanity (which is itself a slave to artifice) produces a grotto (which is art) where necessity enforced a mere passage (that is, one of the mundane events of life not transformed by art). He has essentially refused to be limited by the categorical boundaries that, according to Johnson, should separate ornament from inconvenience. And as the passage cited above demonstrates, Johnson is hard put to know whether to admire or condemn Pope for his transgression. The rest of Johnson's "Life" reflects his ambivalent response to Pope's successful transgression of those boundaries: he admires the poetry, but decries the morals of the poet.

In contrast to the political and social involvement of the eighteenth-century satirists and essayists, the first novelists seem at first glance to share none of the period's great concerns. Rather than attempting to enlist artifice in the service of art, to turn inconvenience into ornament, the early novels throw out the categories of inconvenience and ornament altogether. They are determinedly ordinary. Unlike Pope's poetry, their works offer no glittering surface to be penetrated. They are written in everyday language for a distinctly unliterary audience; they are concerned with the lives of criminals or with domestic tragedies; they seem to be too smugly didactic to participate in any great literary and social concerns.

In fact, the qualities for which the contemporary literary establishment dismissed the novel are precisely the ones that situate it at the heart of the period's desperate attempt to define itself. The great theme of the novel is the individual's effort to define him or herself against the conflicting demands of society, and its supposedly structureless form is simply the old dualistic hierarchy seen from between the poles. The battle that Pope waged in *The Dunciad* and Swift in *Gulliver's Travels* and, for that matter, Gibbon in *The Decline and Fall* between the champions of civilization—of right reason, good taste, and public virtue—and the filth of a life ruled by appetites, passions, and the demands of the body, has been internalized or domesticated in the novel. For example, Richardson's Dullness is named Lovelace; his Yahoos are the Harlowes; the battle for expressive identity takes place in the domestic sphere. Defoe's eternal night is poverty; his protagonists—banished from the domestic sphere—project themselves endlessly outward, redefining expressive selfhood in material terms.

As Ian Watt established definitively some years ago, the form and content of the newly emerging English novel are emblematic of the concerns of the eighteenth century. Watt argues not only that the novel was crucial to the development of a new reading class but also that it incited a new kind of reading—one that "makes us feel that we are in contact not with literature, but with the raw materials of life itself as they are momentarily reflected in the minds of the protagonists."[61] Thus reading became a private experience and a force in the creation of a new kind of individual who prized his or her own uniqueness and whose opinions and desires might well be in conflict with the demands of society. Michael McKeon further develops the idea that the novel is emblematic of eighteenth-century concerns. He stresses, however, that those concerns have to do with the breakdown of epistemological categories, and he is not as interested in the novel's expression or fostering of a new kind of relation between the individual and society.[62]

Defoe and Richardson, who have been criticized variously as

[61]Watt, *Rise of the Novel,* p. 193.
[62]McKeon, *Origins of the English Novel.*

unthinking champions of bourgeois values and as unselfconscious authors who barely had control of their literary tools, in fact shared the Augustans' acute awareness of the fragility of their social world and, like them, believed profoundly in the power of literature continuously to re-create that world. And in their deft manipulation of form and narrative voice, these first novelists deliberately played out the alchemist's struggle that so preoccupied their age. Moreover, they deliberately display for us the techniques by which they resolved that struggle into literature. Like Pope, whose deformity was his gift, or Johnson, who could never reconcile the deformity with the gift and so adopted a perspective above both, Defoe and Richardson lived and wrote by paradox. They found their literary voices by seeming to silence themselves, and they drew—and continue to draw—their readers into their texts' reconstructions of the individual by leaving a gap for us to inhabit.

Clearly then, the strikingly frequent use of a female narrator by the authors of early English novels is evidence that narrative transvestism's meshing of structural and thematic transgressions of established forms was particularly enabling for an exploration of the prevailing issues of the time: the nature and permeability of defining boundaries and the consequences to the individual of transgressing or ignoring them.

Of course, such literary explorations were not confined to the novel. Pope's own efforts to establish the boundaries of what he saw as the simultaneously creative and destructive power of women led him to use a woman's voice or perspective in two of his best-known poems, "The Rape of the Lock" and "Eloisa to Abelard." Yet Pope is not really engaged in narrative transvestism. Although he sometimes writes through a woman's voice, his tone is revealingly ironic. We are always aware of the male poet filling in the words for the female speaker, and the poems finally reconfirm the limitations of the woman's imaginative and social spheres.

Pope's frequent use of the zeugma to point up the incongruity of two very different terms brought together by the same verb stands as an emblem of his use of a female persona. For him, the incongruity or inappropriateness of a male mind in a female body or text is paramount. Eloisa, for example, should not even be writing the name of Abelard. It is only her womanly weakness that causes her to write at all. As "she" states in what starts out to be her own voice but clearly becomes that of a third-person narrator, "In vain lost Eloisa weeps and prays, / Her heart still dictates, and her hand obeys."[63]

In traditional terms, then, a woman's voice is only the voice of marginality and powerlessness, but in the hands of Richardson or Defoe it becomes the key to an alternate view of the self and to recapturing, through the text, the body and all it signifies.

If we situate the birth of the novel as a literary form against this background, then Henry James's description of those "loose baggy monsters" takes on a different valence. The novel was indeed at first without rules as to form. It tended to obscene length, could be divided into any number of chapters, had no rules about rhyme or rhetorical stance, was destined to be read in private and so made intense personal claims on its readers' attention, and so on. The novel was, in fact, the very embodiment of the chaos that this age still quite openly and vehemently identified as dangerously female. In a move that at once thematized and confined that female passion and chaos, however, Defoe and Richardson set themselves the complicated narrative rule that the voice of the novel be a female one. This rhetorical move both affirmed the power of the female voice and usurped or co-opted that power. And if it speaks of nothing else, a narrative form that plays with the categories of gender in this way implies an ironic self-consciousness on the part of the author.

In its response to social upheaval the novel participates in the redefinition of intimate relationships: it structurally redefines

---

[63]Alexander Pope, "Eloisa to Abelard" (1717), in *Poetry and Prose of Alexander Pope*, lines 15–16. On "The Rape of the Lock" as confirming Belinda's marginal status despite her being the prime mover of the poem, see Ellen Pollak, *The Poetics of Sexual Myth: Gender and Ideology in the Verse of Swift and Pope* (Chicago: University of Chicago Press, 1985).

the relationship between author and reader, and it thematically reflects and redefines the terms of intimacy in the family. It does both by transgressing traditional boundaries such as that between the world of the novel and the world of the reader. For Defoe and Richardson, narrative structure clearly moves in two directions: it gives form to the interior of the novel, to the material of the text, and it moves outward to direct the reader's expectations and consequent interpretations of that text.

This double-hinged narrative structure is not by any means new to the novel. The novel engages, however, in thematic debates over precisely this structural device on which it so depends. Society's newly passionate investigation of the nature and definition of the individual gains resonance in the novel's layering of structural and thematic reflections of that investigation. And the point at which these many layers intersect is the male author's transvestite voice.

The novel's development into what Bakhtin calls a heteroglossic form (capable of containing many contradictory voices) that concerns itself primarily with the domestic and emotional life of the individual is intimately related to the early novelists' use of a transvestite narrator. Bakhtin's descriptions of heteroglossia could be descriptions of the process and goals of transvestism:

> Heteroglossia, once incorporated into the novel (whatever the forms for its incorporation), is *another's speech in another's language,* serving to express authorial intentions but in a refracted way. Such speech constitutes a special type of double-voiced discourse. It serves two speakers at the same time and expresses simultaneously two different intentions: the direct intentions of the character who is speaking, and the refracted intention of the author. In such a discourse there are two voices, two meanings and two expressions. And all the while these two voices are dialogically interrelated, they—as it were—know about each other (just as two exchanges in a dialogue know of each other and are structured in this mutual knowledge of each other); it is as if they actually hold conversation with each other.[64]

[64]M. M. Bakhtin, *The Dialogic Imagination,* p. 324. The next passage is from pp. 314–15. All emphases are his.

Bakhtin further notes that narrators use several voices to escape from unitary and singular language: "Such forms open up the possibility of never having to define oneself in language, the possibility of translating one's own intentions from one linguistic system to another, of fusing 'the language of truth' with 'the language of the everday,' of saying 'I am me' in someone else's language, and in my own language, 'I am other.'"

The echoes of Havelock Ellis's definition of the transvestite as putting "too much of 'me' into the 'you' that attracts him" are suggestive of the cycle of authorial assertion and abdication in narrative transvestism.

In the tension between the author's personal imagination and his attempt to realize it in a form in which others can participate, the novel is born. It is as much an arena for the conflict over who shall control meaning as it is a symbolic universe shared by the reader and author. This struggle for connection without surrender takes place between author and reader, self and other, and male and female. Narrative transvestism allows the author to situate these conflicts within the same textual voice, thus concurrently heightening the battle and resolving it into a formal unity.

2

Defoe and *Roxana:*
The Reader as Author

One becomes an author, and in particular an author of fiction, because one can imaginatively create through language a more passionate, more expressive, more vivid and more enduring self than by any other means. By defining the structure of a narrative, one can delineate a protected space within which the world and its population behave as one decrees: events progress toward a discernible conclusion, and the essence of individual characters is revealed along the way. Because this world is a constructed one, its laws and the nature of its characters are unlike those of the world the author actually inhabits. It offers an escape from a generally more confusing reality. Yet this constructed world also offers a guide back to that reality. Thus fiction is by nature paradoxical. Fiction is valuable to its authors and readers alike because it is a fiction, but it relies for its power on our willingness to mistake it—however temporarily—for reality and to see in our own lives a mirror of those constructed lives whose secrets have been revealed to us.

In the same way, the author of such an imaginary reality "becomes" the fictional narrator even while remaining the separate, self-conscious author. Defoe, for example, takes great pains to make his narratives appear to be seamless, as if there were no distance between the author and the narrator, as if Daniel Defoe, the trueborn Englishman, had also been on the island with

Robinson Crusoe and in Newgate with Moll Flanders. And of course Daniel Defoe is Robinson Crusoe on that island—but it is an island of his own imagining, and he makes us aware of the work of his imagination even while he attempts to draw us into the fiction. One of his primary tools for achieving this double goal is the impressive display of realistic details that characterizes so much of his work. He offers us this realistic detail as both the content and the structure of his autobiographers' narratives: we are regaled with precise accounts of the goods Moll Flanders steals and with a catalogue of her false narrative starts, her retellings, her embellishments, and her lapses. Thus these same accounts and catalogues that are the stuff of Defoe's fiction entice us into mistaking that fiction for reality. As such they are both tool and display: the author is exhibiting the sleight of hand by which fiction becomes a temporary reality, and reality a tool of the fiction writer. If Defoe is successful, if we are enticed by the strange hybrid of fiction willingly to suspend disbelief, then while we read, we too become hybrid creatures—real participants in a fictional world.

Part of the power of fiction stems from the very temporariness of its illusion. We agree, for a while, to tolerate the contradiction that an author is simultaneously herself or himself as well as someone else in a fictional narrative. And this ephemeral character who exists between the covers of a book often comes to seem more complexly human and certainly more knowable than anyone outside the text. Fiction thus provides a protected space for the reader as well as for the author: we can more fully participate with this unknown author in an illusion because we know the illusion has distinct boundaries. We can close the book at any time; we can withdraw; we can deny that we and the author are engaged in any kind of shared enterprise at all. The task of the fiction writer is suggestively to transgress all of those boundaries that are so necessary to the reader even while recognizing that the fiction would not exist at all without them.

Any author takes many twists and turns along the route toward establishing a creative relationship with his or her readers through the text. We respond differently to a text such as Swift's *Tale of a Tub,* whose author continually undercuts his own power, than we do to one like *Tom Jones* or even *Tristram Shandy,* whose authors display all the tricks of their trade only to reassert their imaginative power over us. Swift brings us rather unsettlingly close to the agonies and ambiguities of the writer's attempts to organize the world, and he has a startling habit of revealing the abyss of unstable meanings beneath the elegant surface of his works. Sterne and Fielding, despite their very different narrative styles, both appear eager to remind us that we are not, in fact, authors as they are. We are readers, and our role is to follow along, to be clever enough to laugh at the jokes and to admire the artistry as artistry.

Defoe takes a different tack altogether: he requires neither our indulgence nor our subservience to his authorial power. In fact, his authorial power is not at issue at all. He clearly displays both the extent and the limits of that power when, in his guise as an autobiographical narrator of true events, he captivates us, only to frustrate our desire for a linear, unambiguous tale with a clear moral message. In each of his novels Defoe creates a compellingly detailed imaginary world and then leaves us alone with his narrators and their self-contradictions. Consequently, we are rather roughly thrown back upon our own resources as readers. These novels require that we actively participate in their narrators' efforts at autobiography. Gradually we become accomplices to their attempts to form an explanation and a justification for their lives out of the "raw material" of their adventures.

Virginia Woolf notes this discomfiting effect of Defoe's novels when she observes that they are frustrating to read ("he thwarts us and flouts us at every turn") and that his paradoxical invention of true facts produces results that we don't expect from novels: "Before we open the book we have perhaps vaguely sketched out the kind of pleasure we expect it to give us. We read; and we are rudely contradicted on every page. There are no sunsets and no sunrises; there is no solitude and no soul. There is, on the contrary, staring us full in the face nothing but a large earthenware pot."[1]

Woolf nicely identifies Defoe's designs upon his readers: "Finally, that is to say, we are forced to drop our own preconceptions and to accept what Defoe himself wishes to give us." Often, however, critics have shrunk from the notion that Defoe was exerting some authorial power over his readers, and have instead concentrated on accumulating the evidence to support a claim that Defoe simply didn't know what he was doing. His novels are frustrating to read, they assert, because Defoe lost control of his narrators and couldn't keep track of the details he so irritatingly accumulated. This strategy neatly confines all literary critical issues within the boundaries of the text and precisely sidesteps the demand that Defoe's novels make upon us: that we transgress with him the various boundaries between author, character, and reader. When we examine the interchange between structure and theme, and between narrative and character, we come to recognize that Defoe spent so little time developing "realistic" relationships between his characters because the relationship that interested him was the one between author and reader. This creative exchange between the structure of his texts and those contradictions or ambiguities that manifest themselves in his characters and his plots is the locus of Defoe's artistry, and of his power over precisely those readers who fail to recognize that he exercises any artistry at all.

If we examine the complicated first-person narrator Defoe habitually used for his novels, we can see a clear example of how he merged structure with content to draw the reader into the cooperative venture that is the text. Each of these narrators' efforts to make moral and emotional sense of a dizzying array of adventures leads him or her to cling in turn to notions of God, fate, chance, or economic determinism to lend coherence to his

---

[1]Virginia Woolf, "Robinson Crusoe," in *The Second Common Reader* (New York: Harcourt, Brace & World, 1960), p. 45. The next quotation I cite is from p. 46.

or her life. But with the resources available within the boundaries of the text, the narrative "I" can establish only a temporary hierarchy of cause and effect, good and evil, and past and future. Each one finally makes a direct appeal to the reader—to a source of knowledge outside the text—to sort out just how much money was made and lost, how many children were born, how much rice was planted, and just what the moral imperatives of any individual's progress through these events might be.

Moll Flanders, Robinson Crusoe, Roxana, and the H. F. of the *Journal of the Plague Year,* for example, all tell their own stories, looping their tales through the narrative present they share with their readers, through the historical present of the events they're relating, and through the eternal present of the moral consequences of their actions. In addition, each of these narrators makes liberal use of some form of direct address to her or his readers; we are explicitly invited to accompany these autobiographers on their retrospective journeys through the vagaries of fortune to spiritual or material redemption, or both.

The invitation is a seductive one. The narrators infect us with their urgent need to tell their stories, and they overwhelm our skepticism with details, with elaborately intricate circumstantial evidence designed to lend concreteness—if not realism—to their tales. In general, we are taken in. Captivated by the urgency of the ever-shifting present tense, disarmed by the details of each of several versions of any single event, we disregard the teller and give ourselves over to the tale. Defoe's narrators seem to be wholly transparent; their fumbles, digressions, and repetitions serve to point our attention toward their adventures rather than the manner of their telling. None of these narrators has any literary pretensions. Instead, each one seems to say, I am but a simple and uneducated soul and can only relate in a straightforward and unadorned manner the extraordinary adventures that have befallen me. Thus is literary criticism effectively disarmed. We respond to Crusoe's inconsistencies, Moll's transparent greed, Roxana's frustratingly vague accounts of children born and fortunes earned and lost, and H. F.'s always presaged but ever-delayed escape from London as evidence of their characters and of their human flaws rather than as narrative devices.

In this way we are not taken in so much by Robinson Crusoe or by Roxana as by Defoe himself. As we search out the flaws in his characters, we willingly accede to his pretense that no author stands behind the characters. Because Defoe isn't an obviously ironic metanarrative presence, we lose track of him. We see only the narrator creating—more or less convincingly—the tale, not the author creating both narrator and tale. That is, even though we know that the same author wrote each of these "autobiographies," while we are reading we believe that the narrator and Defoe are effectively one and the same. We may know that he did not experience all of Moll Flanders's adventures, but we believe that the limits of her narrative self-consciousness coincide with his limits as an artist. For example, while Moll is complaining about parents who make their well-dressed children easy prey for pickpockets like herself, or Crusoe is telling us about hoarding the gold he finds, even though it's useless to him, we are struck by the ironies of such self-serving moralizing, but we are not aware that Defoe has led us to this perspective on his narrators. Instead, we think that Defoe is as inconsistent as Crusoe, as much a moral relativist as Moll, and as lacking in a sense of the ridiculous as both.

In the section on *Moll Flanders* in *The Rise of the Novel*, Ian Watt very nicely dismisses any notion that Defoe might have been an artist or even a particularly self-conscious craftsman:

> Th[e] somewhat primitive aspect of Defoe's narrative technique is partly a reflection of the nature of his basic literary purpose—to produce a convincing likeness to the autobiographical memoir of a real person. . . .
>
> The most remarkable thing about the prose of the passage is perhaps the fact that it is Defoe's usual style. No previous author's normal way of writing could so credibly have passed for the characteristic utterance of such an uneducated person as Moll Flanders. . . .
>
> There is probably no episode in Moll Flanders where the motivation is unconvincing, but for somewhat damaging reasons—few

of the situations confronting Defoe's heroine call for any more complex discrimination than those of Pavlov's dog: Defoe makes us admire the speed and resolution of Moll's reactions to profit or danger; and if there are no detailed psychological analyses, it is because they would be wholly superfluous.[2]

In this way, Watt effectively takes *Moll Flanders* out of the realm of literature. He declares that Moll is simply Defoe dressed in a skirt and that her story is in effect an autobiography because Defoe was incapable of writing anything else: "There is certainly nothing in *Moll Flanders* which clearly indicates that Defoe sees the story differently from the heroine" (122). Watt abandons any investigation of the text as literature in favor of his social analysis of the rise of the novel. For him, the text itself becomes an instrument in that rise, and he praises Defoe as a genuine spokesman for a new reading public. Defoe wrote effectively, Watt claims, for those of his time whose views of social relations and whose expectations of literature were as limited as his own.

Following Watt, critics have often focused on Defoe's novels as historical or sociological texts, thereby making insignificant the complexities of narrative and the seeming inconsistencies of character. Other recent critical approaches have given Defoe more credit for his artistry. David Marshall, for example, admires Defoe as a self-conscious artist who cleverly manipulates his various personae in a theatrical exploration of the instability of identity. Marshall sees the characters' patterns of reticence and revelation as a mirror for Defoe's own reticence; he reads *Moll Flanders* and *Roxana* as autobiographical fictions, not fictional autobiographies.[3]

---

[2]Watt, *Rise of the Novel*, pp. 98, 99, 100, 108.

[3]David Marshall, *The Figure of Theater: Shaftesbury, Defoe, Adam Smith, and George Eliot* (New York: Columbia University Press, 1986). The distinction between autobiographical fiction and fictional autobiography is on p. 112. Marshall's identification of Defoe with his characters causes him to ignore the more complex relationship between the author's reticence and that played out by his narrators. In essence, he sees Roxana's reluctance to be seen as evidence that Defoe was also reluctant to show himself. I see it as one way Defoe involves the reader in the novel's creation of character. Similarly, Marshall doesn't deal with the complexities involved in the author's choice of a female narrator for his autobiography. As a result, he doesn't

Defoe deliberately leads us to believe that the limits of his narrators' self-awareness are also his own limits. In other words, he deftly obscures the significance of a fact that he never denies: an author stands behind these narrators, and these are biographies of imagined lives. To this end, Defoe never intrudes a clear editorial voice which might make obvious any ironic or other critical approach he means us to take to his fictions.

Criticism that loses sight of the author tends also to ignore the complexities of its own relationship to the text. When not provided with a sense of deliberate authorial intention, the critic or reader likely falls prey to the temptation to fill the gap with his or her own image. Defoe, of course, counted on precisely the pull of this vacuum to involve us in his texts. He does his best to make us unselfconscious participants. He has upon occasion had rather spectacular success. James Sutherland, for example, in a remarkable moment of self-revelation, claims that Roxana, unlike Moll, "at least gives her various men good value for their money."[4]

Defoe's reputation for "the most amazing talent on record for telling lies"[5] should be seen as a tribute to the subtlety of his narrative presence. Instead, his talent for lying has sometimes

---

sufficiently consider the differences between the structures of the narrator's story and the author's. The narrator's revelations are governed by the author's own cycle of asserting authority and then abdicating it; what Marshall identifies as a pattern of self-concealment I identify as the self-creating process of narrative transvestism. For other works dealing with the tricky relationship between Defoe and his narrative personae, see David Blewett, *Defoe's Art of Fiction: Robinson Crusoe, Moll Flanders, Colonel Jack, and Roxana* (Toronto: University of Toronto Press, 1979); Leopold Damrosch, Jr., "Defoe as Ambiguous Impersonator," *Modern Philology* 71 (1973):153–59; and Irvin Ehrenpreis, "Personae," in Carroll Camden, ed., *Restoration and Eighteenth-Century Literature: Essays in Honor of Alan Dugald McKillop* (Chicago: University of Chicago Press, 1963), pp. 25–37. For works that take into account that some of those personae are women, see Nancy K. Miller, *Heroine's Text*, and John J. Richetti, "The Portrayal of Women in Restoration and Eighteenth-Century Literature," in Marlene Springer, ed., *What Manner of Woman: Essays on English and American Life and Literature* (New York: New York University Press, 1977), pp. 65–97.

[4]James Sutherland, *Defoe* (London: Methuen, 1937, rpt. 1950), p. 239.

[5]Leslie Stephen, "Defoe's Novels," in *Hours in a Library* (New York: Putnam, 1904), p. 4. Cited in John J. Richetti, *Defoe's Narratives: Situations and Structures* (Oxford: Clarendon Press, 1975), p. 5, n. 7.

led critics to dismiss the rich and deliberate ambiguity of his prose fictions. Anxious not to be taken in by what Virginia Woolf calls Defoe's "genius for fact,"[6] they have asserted, for example, that the author was himself ignorant of the irony that Moll Flanders's repentance is fueled by her accumulation of wealth, and that *The Shortest Way With Dissenters* is the work of a politically naive satirist rather than a piece of deliberately rabble-rousing propaganda.

The assumption here is that *The Shortest Way* could not be *both* satire and rabble-rousing propaganda and that Defoe couldn't have written so convincingly as Moll if he also saw through or beyond her. In fact, much of Defoe's achievement is this double vision through which he can both see the world as Moll and see the world to which she is blind. And it is precisely this double vision that characterizes fiction as fiction: the author both is and is not wholly identified with her or his characters. The writer simultaneously inhabits the position of the narrator and of the author with a sharp eye out for his or her audience and for the limits of our willing participation in his or her fiction.

Focusing on the transvestite structure of Defoe's narrative allows me to join the enduring questions about Defoe's control over his novels and his use of irony to an investigation of how his novels are engaged in the period's reformulation of gender categories. In detailing the contradictions, tensions, and continual revisions embedded within Roxana's seemingly effortless and unstoppable narrative of her great amorous and monetary successes and of her final disquietude, I show how the split in Roxana's own voice meshes with the novel's thematic debate over the true nature of woman. Roxana's conviction that she is a man—and an articulate creature—when she has money, but a woman when she is helpless and silenced by her passion for her daughter Susan, precisely mirrors Defoe's own progress back and forth—in this transvestite narrative—between man and woman and between self and other. The imperatives of narrative

[6]Woolf, "Robinson Crusoe," p. 48.

and gender further converge in Roxana's relationships to her maid Amy and to her daughter Susan, and it is here that we can see most clearly how Defoe draws the reader into his narrative project so that we gather the fragments—of both character and novel—into a whole.

The Defects of Performance

Like Defoe's other novels, *Roxana* pretends to be an autobiographical narrative, written, of course, in the first-person voice. According to the Preface (whose author, as we shall see, is both mysterious and slippery), *"The History of this* Beautiful Lady, *is to speak for itself."*[7] In this odd formulation history has a voice, but the Beautiful Lady does not. And even her history, which is supposedly speaking for itself, comes to us after it has been filtered through several men who are identified only by their literary functions in this supposedly entirely historical and literary text: they are the Relator, the Writer, and the "I," who at times supersedes them both.

The Relator himself alerts us to the layers of mediation in the narrative and to how these layers necessarily complicate our readerly response. With a small demonstration he reminds us that these multiple narrative layers present us with a choice: we can respond to any one voice (if indeed we can trace one) as Roxana's "real" voice, or we can participate in the process by which a more complicated voice creates itself.[8]

If it [the story] *is not as Beautiful as the Lady herself is reported to be; if it is not as diverting as the Reader can desire, and much more than he can reasonably expect, and if all the most diverting Parts of it are not adapted*

---

[7]Daniel Defoe, *Roxana: The Fortunate Mistress,* ed. Jane Jack (New York: Oxford University Press, 1981), p. 1. Future page numbers will be in the body of the text. All italics are Defoe's.

[8]John Richetti, in *Defoe's Narratives,* nicely calls this discerning "the patterns in the process of emerging." He goes on to state the intent of his book on Defoe: "My hope is to catch the fictions as they rise and mark the self as it flies with them" (20).

to the Instruction and Improvement of the Reader, the Relator says, *it must be from the Defect of his Performance; dressing up the Story in worse Cloaths than the* Lady, *whose Words he speaks, prepar'd it for the World.* (1)

The Relator's object lesson here is essentially a demonstration of narrative power. What Defoe gives us with one voice or perspective or incident, he can take away or complicate with another. In this instance the Relator proceeds, clause by clause, to deflate our readerly hopes even before we have had the chance to form any. The Relator tells us that this story might not be as beautiful as the Lady is reported to be, thus oddly equating her physical beauty with the more abstract qualities of the story. His use of the word "reported," however, reduces the Lady's beauty to an abstraction (if not to hearsay), while we hold the concrete embodiment of her story in our hands. It seems that we are being asked to accept this story as a satisfying substitute for the Lady herself. The Relator then elaborates on what that might mean: the Lady's story (and, by inference, the Lady herself) can never satisfy our desire for diversion, although it (she) might divert us more than we could reasonably expect. Moreover, where the story is most successful at diverting us, it might be least "adapted to [our] Instruction and Improvement." So it is not in our best interest for the story even partially to satisfy our inappropriate desires and our unreasonable expectations. But neither possibility—that the story won't satisfy us or that it will satisfy us at some moral cost—is the Lady's fault. Rather, both possibilities result from a defect in the Relator's performance, for he has dressed "up [her] Story in worse Cloaths than the Lady, whose Words he speaks, prepar'd it for the world."

This is a very complex apology, complicated still further by its strange syntax. Either way you read it, the Lady's story is treated as a bodily entity in need of clothing, whose literary equivalent is words. But if the Relator's words are worse clothes for her story than were the Lady's *words*, then the clothing of expressive language is accessible to both men and women; in fact, the

Relator might have used it to less effect than the Lady. If, however, with his version of her words the Relator has dressed the Lady's story in worse clothes than she herself *wore,* then she has access only to the language of the body and to actual rather than metaphorical clothing. If this is so, then she cannot tell her own story, and she is all the more vulnerable to the defects of his performance. But, as with the slippery transfer of the characteristics of physical and narrative beauty that I noted above, here it is difficult to tell when "words" and "clothes" are metaphorically the same thing and when they are being used to preserve the distinction between narrator and subject. What might have been a simple acknowledgment that the Lady's story has been transformed by the Relator's telling of it has become a subtly disturbing lesson about the complex exchanges between tale, teller, and audience, or material, artistry, and interpretation.

Thus the Relator establishes the terms of our readerly response: he has told us what we expect from this work; that we might not get what we expect; that if we did get it, that might not be so good for us; that if we don't get it (or if it's not so good for us), that's not the beautiful Lady's fault but simply the reflection of his less beautiful performance of her history.

If a reader paused (something Defoe never encourages us to do) to examine the complexities of this first paragraph of the Preface to *Roxana,* she would find what amounts to a primer to the restless migrations of Defoe's narrative stance in the novel and to the demands that continual movement makes on the reader. We are, for example, asked to accept the paradoxical assertion that the existence of the Lady is questionable but that her history is genuine. Defoe never resolves this paradox. He simply abandons it in favor of another one: that even though he is speaking the Lady's own words, his performance of her story may be flawed.

Obviously, if he has "dressed up" her story, then the Relator can't also be speaking the Lady's own words. And if there might be "defects" in his "performance" of her story, one wonders why he has substituted his worse clothes for her better ones. Why not let the Lady speak for herself?

The equation of words with clothes is, of course, one clue to why the Lady is not to be allowed to speak for herself: this is a transvestite narrative; there is no Lady. There is only a male Relator, dressing himself in a lady's clothes and telling his story as if it were hers. The narrative fiction of the Lady and her true experiences is, like the real-world transvestite's feminine attire, a creative device. In narrative, this device enables the creation of a structure within which self and other (author and character or author and reader) can safely merge temporarily in mutually defining opposition. That same defining and protective structure allows the author to be self-conscious about the very device he is using and to reflect the implications of his own relationship to his text in the relationships between his characters and, most of all, in the response he elicits from his readers.

This playful and unsettling self-awareness is precisely what Defoe establishes through the contradictory assertions and the sudden reversals of his Preface to *Roxana*. Defoe's play is unsettling for readers because it asks us to allow him those contradictions and reversals. To participate in *Roxana*, we must be willing to resist the anxious desire to fix Defoe reassuringly in one single narrative perspective. If we do resist that desire, then we gain "much more [diversion] than [we] can reasonably expect." We gain what Defoe himself gains through these complicated narrative maneuvers: participation in and understanding of the process by which an individual defines herself or himself.

But even if we recognize and acquiesce to this narrative strategy, we always find ourselves one step behind Defoe. For example, just as we begin to sort out the implications of the Relator's relationship to the Lady, Defoe further complicates matters by undermining the Relator just as he has already undercut the Lady and her history. It turns out that the Relator, like the Lady, only exists in the third person; neither ever speaks to us directly. In the first quotation cited in this section, some disembodied voice asserts that "the Relator says." In the next paragraph Defoe draws our attention to this seemingly inconsequential formulation:

> He takes the Liberty to say, That this Story differs from most of the Modern Performances of this Kind, tho' some of them have been with a very good Reception in the World: I say, It differs from them in this Great and Essential Article, Namely, That the Foundation of This is laid in Truth of Fact; and so the Work is not a Story, but a History. (1)

Who is this "I" who is making more explicit the claims of the "He" who is relating the story of this Beautiful Lady in her own words if not in her own clothes? More importantly, what is his relationship to—and what are his claims on—the reader to whom this Preface is addressed?

The Relator of the first paragraph started out referring to the "history" of the lady and closed with a reference to her "story." The "I" of the second paragraph asserts that the work "is not a Story, but a History." The reader is given no clue to the relative merits of these claims nor even to the speakers' respective definitions of "story" and "history." Instead, the majority of the second and third paragraphs of the Preface is occupied with an explanation of the necessity of concealing "Names and Persons," and an assertion that the "History" is no less valuable for this concealment. Presumably it is still the voice of the "I," who goes on to explain the necessity of anonymity.

The fourth paragraph of the Preface begins, however, "*The Writer says, He was particularly acquainted with this Lady's First Husband*" (1). Is the Writer the same as the Relator? And who is in a position to refer to the Writer in the third person? Is it the unidentified "I" from whom we've already heard? Is "I" Defoe's unadorned voice? Whatever the answers, they carry us to an ever-increasing remove from the Lady and her story.

Defoe implicitly acknowledges the risk he runs of forfeiting our involvement in and our credulous attention to the Lady's story when he calls in the Writer to vouch for the truth of the first part of the Lady's story, which "*may, he hopes, be a Pledge for the*

Credit of the rest, tho' [it] could not so well be vouch'd for as the First"
(2). This characteristically ambiguous assertion of support for
the Lady is made still more ambiguous by the claim (by some
voice other than the Writer's) that, *"yet, as she has told it herself, we
have the less Reason to question the Truth of that Part also"* (2). Of
course, "she" hasn't told the story herself, and if her word were
enough to establish the truth of her story, these troops of men
would not have been called in to vouch for her (or rather, to
vouch for the existence of her first husband) and to dress up her
story for public consumption. Everyone (except the Lady, from
whom we have yet to hear directly) has apologized for the
inadequacies of the narrative to come even while vouching for
the truth of its content. We are left to conclude that the Lady
whose story this is, after all, has served well as a receptacle for
experience, but that she is not reliably able to articulate or formu-
late that experience.

The Preface goes on to assert that, although the Lady *"met with
unexpected Success in all her wicked Courses,"* the intent of the
narrative is to expose vice, *"and if the Reader makes a wrong Use of
the Figures, the Wickedness is his own"* (2). It ends with the noble
assertion that *"we make no Question, the Story, however meanly told,
will find a Passage to his best Hours; and be read both with Profit and
Delight"* (3). "We" is perhaps the most accurate pronoun used in
the Preface to refer to the presenters of this tale, but this last
assertion that the reader cannot help but profit from the story
contradicts the earlier one that the reader's own wickedness
might cause him to "make a wrong use of the figures." Defoe
could hardly have laid out more explicitly his strategy to elicit
proper readerly participation in his novel: he intends both to
tempt and to frustrate our desires, to manipulate us and to make
us responsible for acquiescing to that manipulation.

The Preface occupies barely more than two pages of the text,
but Defoe's shifts from "the Relator" to "I" to "the Writer" to
"we" have allowed him variously to assert that: this is Roxana's
own story; the male Relator is responsible for the "defects" of the
story; the story is a true one, for part of which, at least, the male

Writer can vouch—and hence that it is the creation of history; but finally that the reader has the power to misread the story and so make it her or his own in spite of the combined creative efforts of Roxana, the Writer, and History to interpret that story for us. Thus, although we have been flooded with answers, we are still left with the question, Whose story or voice is this?

One possibility is, of course, that it is no one person's story or voice. Rather it is the amalgam of voices available to Defoe as he moves through the creative stages of narrative transvestism. Another possibility is that it is indeed Roxana's story and Roxana's voice that we hear—whoever Roxana (or, as she styles herself, a "Roxana") might be. Both are true; Roxana's narrative is at once the record of Defoe's literary process and the expression of a fictional character who has her own integrity. We are aware of each of these separate truths at different points in our own developing involvement with the narrative.

Our first impression is that a "Roxana" has no integrity at all. She is a creature of wandering garrulousness, a stranger to boundaries of any sort, and, in particular, no respecter of narrative divisions. Like so much of Defoe's prose, *Roxana* seems at first reading to have no structure at all. Except for the three-page preface, the book has no divisions. And, although Roxana's monologue has a beginning, it doesn't have a real ending—she simply trails off. The narrative is more cyclical than linear. It is driven by Roxana's search for a self and a home, and as both the narrative structure and the plot demonstrate, that search is a self-reflexive and never-ending one.

Her story significantly begins with an event that makes her something of a hybrid creature, not quite an English woman and not quite a French one: "I was born, *as my Friends told me*, at the City of POICTIERS, in the province, or County of POICTOU in *France*, from whence I was brought to *England* by my Parents, who fled for their Religion about the Year 1683, when the Protestants were Banish'd from France by the Cruelty of their Persecutors" (5). Typically, Roxana immediately contradicts herself: she offers economic hardship as another reason for her parents' emigration. This contradiction is the pattern of her narrative: no sooner has she made a statement or recounted an adventure than she contradicts herself or revises her interpretation of it. And these same reversals characterize the larger structure of the novel as well: an episode builds to a high level of dramatic tension and is then abandoned; Roxana embarks on a trajectory and then reverses herself. She interrupts the present to revise the past or to prepare for future events so often that chronology is hopelessly confused.

The novel keeps doubling back on itself. At the end as at the beginning, Roxana is a hybrid creature made up of parts of Susan, parts of Amy, and parts of the reader. She collapses when Susan disappears and Amy refuses to explain her part in that disappearance. But that collapse is not obviously different from any of the previous collapses (including the one that begins the novel) from which Roxana has regrouped and gone on.

> Here, after some few Years of flourishing, and outwardly happy Circumstances, I fell into a dreadful Course of Calamities, and Amy also; the very Reverse of our former Good Days; the Blast of Heaven seem'd to follow the Injury done the poor Girl, by us both; and I was brought so low again, that my Repentance seem'd to be only the Consequence of my Misery, as my Misery was of my Crime. (330)

This is not so much an ending as a circling back to the beginning of the narrative. At several other points in the novel Roxana has made this same kind of declaration of defeat and imminent demise, only to embark on a re-creation of her narrative self through the temporary merging with some other, a merging that for her always sparks a flurry of activity. And she has "ended" her story before, pointing out to us the moral to come, only to plunge into the particulars of her adventures once more. She does this rather strikingly at the very beginning of her tale: "In a word, all was Misery and Distress, the Face of Ruin was every where to be seen; we had eaten up almost every thing, and little remain'd, unless, like one of the pitiful Women of *Jerusalem*, I should eat up my very Children themselves" (17).

Roxana does end up destroying her daughter to preserve

herself—or rather Amy does it for her as, on this occasion of Roxana's abandonment by her husband, Amy speaks for her: "Amy told them all my Circumstances, and set them forth in such moving Terms, and so to the Life, that I could not upon any Terms have done it like her myself" (18).

It is always some outside agent who rescues Roxana from her despair, and that intervention seems to recall her each time to her narrative purpose, as if her collapse were a mere digression. She dutifully abandons her interpretive and moralizing flights in favor of a supposedly straightforward account of events or, as she puts it, to return "to my own Story" (207 and passim).

Thus, every seeming conclusion is but a pause in the continuing cycle of assertion, defeat, and reengagement by which character is created. And it would seem that the only difference between Roxana's final defeat and all the interim ones is that the novel abruptly ends with this defeat. In fact, that final despair eventually reveals itself as qualitatively different from the others: it is a despair born of moral discomfort rather than of a financial or pragmatic setback, and that moral quality stems from Roxana's failure as a mother. I return to both these issues; here it is important to note that nothing in Roxana's account of her final paralysis alerts us to its finality; the differences from her earlier crises are implied through the conjunction of events rather than through any quality of the narrative voice. In fact, Roxana's tone is hesitant and confused, which suggests not that she has reached a conclusion but that she simply doesn't know where to go next. She might well be waiting for the usual external impetus that would prompt her to embark once more upon the task of self-creation.

This process of self-creation takes place on several levels in *Roxana*. On the level of the plot it entails reengagement with the oppressive circumstances of what John Richetti defines as "the central problem that [Roxana] solves in her book, the loss of self attendant upon being merely a woman" (*Defoe's Narratives*, 195). The activities by which Roxana creates herself are the purposeful accumulation of wealth and the accidental production of children. Wealth makes her more confident that she can act in the world; when she has control of her money she is a "Masculine in her politick Capacity" (148). Children, who terrify her, are an unfortunate by-product of her method of acquiring wealth and of her need to borrow selfhood from the men with whom she so emphatically refuses to merge her finances.

On the level of the "autobiography," we see Roxana's attempt to define a self in the split or contradictions in her narrative. Here again Richetti's exposition of how difficult it is for an individual character in Defoe's works to establish and maintain the boundaries of the self is an astute one. But then, implying that Roxana's quest has been a successful one, he ignores how divided she is against herself:

> Defoe's novels are not, as is sometimes asserted, naive celebrations of individual possibility. They are most accurately described as dramatizations of what can be called the individualist dilemma. They communicate by their arrangements and strategies an implicit grasp of the tangled relationships between the free self and the social and ideological realities which that self seems to require. What they show us as we read is character carefully separating itself from that unsatisfactory tangle of private and public, personal and social, and establishing an unimpeachable selfhood, at least in the privileged space of the narrative. (*Defoe's Narratives*, 17)

Like Roxana herself, Richetti assumes that the threats to a stable identity are external ones, that the self could be "free" if only it could fight off the need to be anchored in and reaffirmed by "social and ideological realities." Roxana acts out this fantasy of the free self in her quest for money and her denial of her daughter's emotional claims upon her. But even in "the privileged space of the narrative," neither one gets her "an unimpeachable selfhood." They each do, at times, get her a kind of provisional selfhood. Roxana has a sporadic ability to act in the world, to accumulate wealth, and to give birth to children. But her responses to events (whether they're external, like the Prince's repentance, or internal, like her impassioned response to Susan) are unpredictable, and she is always in danger of subsiding into passivity. In fact, Roxana's "self" is remarkably unaffected by her adventures. She doesn't learn from one crisis how to deal with the next; neither does her own quest for unimpeachable selfhood allow her to identify or empathize with Susan's desperate desire to fix her origins—to anchor herself in Roxana as Roxana does in Amy.

When Roxana's story trails off at the end of the book, she is as baffled by her fate and by her relationship to others as she is at the beginning when she portrays Amy as the faithful friend who sustains her, and as the devil who destroyed her:

> Poor Amy and I had drank nothing but Water for many Weeks, and indeed, I have often wonder'd at the faithful Temper of the poor Girl; for which I but ill requited her at last. (26)

> Had I now had my Sences about me, and had my Reason not been overcome by the powerful Attraction of so kind, so beneficent a Friend; had I consulted Conscience and Virtue, I shou'd have repell'd this Amy, however faithful and honest to me in other things, as a Viper, and Engine of the Devil; . . . The ignorant Jade's Argument, That he had brought me out of the Hands of the Devil, by which she meant the Devil of Poverty and Distress, shou'd have been a powerful Motive to me, not to plunge myself into the Jaws of Hell, and into the Power of the real Devil, in Recompence for that Deliverance; . . . Amy had but too much Rhetorick in this Cause; (38–39)

Roxana is something of a spectator of her own life; narrative and experience don't impinge upon each other the way they do for the letter writers in *Clarissa*. She is, in fact, so far removed from her adventures that she frequently slips into a kind of third-person narrative of them. She is, moreover, equally removed from her narrative of those adventures. She never listens to herself; she is unperturbed by the contradictions and gaps in her tale. As the Preface made clear, the Lady is simply a container for experience; she can neither articulate it coherently nor interpret it.

In the second passage I cite above, for example, Roxana interrupts her condemnation of Amy and her seductive rhetoric to announce both that "Poverty was my Snare" and that "Besides this, I was young, handsome, and with all the Mortifications I had met with, was vain." These are the traces of two other narratives which simply emerge from the details of events from time to time and then are resubmerged. Roxana tells us several concurrent life histories: the tale of a helpless woman victimized by economic necessity and a sinful maid; the tale of a "calculating adventuress who finds that she can secure a life of luxury by trading on her personal charms";[9] a moral tale of a successful criminal made miserable by her conscience; and a tale that is hardly coherent at all but which seems to express the difficulties of creating a coherent life history.

Clearly Roxana's narrative is not really a monologue at all; it has embedded within it several different voices and perspectives on her story. Roxana herself never puts the pieces together—or indeed even acknowledges the divisions—but we do, so that the accumulation of self and of self-consciousness is the reader's activity, not the character's. For the reader, however, narrative and experience are one and the same. Consequently, we are the ones who benefit from the slow accretion of experience and who work to a selfhood that is unimpeachable by virtue of its fluidity and its tolerance for contradiction. For example, it becomes clear to us in the course of the narrative that Roxana and Amy are hardly separate characters at all and that although Roxana tells her story in the first person, she is often marginal to the tale. She remains passive while Amy, various husbands and lovers, and Susan propel the events of her life.

The split that takes the explicit forms of Lady, Relator, Writer, and "I" in the Preface is also in evidence in Roxana's obsessive doubling back upon events to tell them again with a different moral and interpretive overlay. In particular, that split is often

---

[9]John Robert Moore, *Daniel Defoe: Citizen of the Modern World* (Chicago: University of Chicago Press, 1958), p. 249.

manifested in the presence of an incompletely integrated moral commentary upon Roxana's chosen route to survival: whoredom.

Thus, even as she succumbs to Amy's arguments that "Honesty is out of the Question, when Starving is the Case" (28), Roxana recites a creed of absolute right and wrong: "for, without question, a Woman ought rather to die, than to prostitute her Virtue and Honour, let the Temptation be what it will" (29). Since Roxana's very next sentence begins, "But to return to my Story," it is clear that this moral code has little relation to or effect upon her experience. It does, however, affect the reader. We experience the dislocation between Roxana's actions and her expressed moral code as a contradiction and so exert ourselves to resolve it. On the level of the tale, however, the two perspectives or two voices don't clash so much as they coexist. One simply gives way to the other, and as Defoe did in the Preface, Roxana moves on.

> I had no Inclination to be a Wife again, . . . I found, that a Wife is treated with Indifference, a Mistress with a strong Passion; a Wife is look'd upon, as but an Upper-Servant, a Mistress is a Sovereign; a Wife must give up all she has . . . whereas a Mistress makes the Saying true, *that what the Man has*, is hers, and *what she has*, is her own; the Wife bears a thousand Insults, and is forc'd to sit still and bear it, or part and be undone; a Mistress insulted, helps herself immediately, and takes another.
>
> These were my wicked Arguments for Whoring, for I never set against them the Difference another way; . . . A Wife appears boldly and honourably with her Husband; . . . The Whore sculks about in Lodgings; . . . but my Business is History. (132–33)

This moralizing voice is a constant of Roxana's narrative, and it is the last voice we hear from her as she ends her story with references to her Misery and her Crime. Because this moralizing voice has no effect on the tale but only on the reading of the tale, we often experience it as a third-person interruption of Roxana's story. We could identify those interruptions as the defects of the Relator's performance of that story, but of course the performance—defects and all—is the story. Just as there is no Lady independent of the Relator who impersonates her, Roxana's story would not exist without these "interruptions." When she says, "Being to give my own Character, I must be excus'd to give it as impartially as possible, and as if I was speaking of another-body; *and the Sequel will lead you to judge whether I flatter myself or no*" (6), she makes it clear that the split between experience and narrative is what allows "her" to speak at all. Like the Relator borrowing the Lady's clothes, Roxana speaks of herself as if she were "another-body." And her ability to become another body, to assume other costumes (such as the Quaker dress in which she tries to hide from Susan) and even other personalities (she is a hard-bargaining business woman with the Dutch merchant and a passive bauble, a "Roxana" for the Prince), is what allows Roxana to survive. Thus the mutable self of Roxana's narrative is mirrored, on the level of the plot, by these disguises, and both these in turn mirror the enabling transvestite structure of Defoe's novel.

"I wou'd be a *Man-Woman*"

We've seen that Roxana's narrative, which at first seems to be an uninterrupted flow of wandering garrulousness, is actually divided against itself in several ways. The first-person voice has no stable inhabitant, so it presents us with conflicting versions of events and of their moral consequences. As readers we are free to—indeed often feel compelled to—dissolve these divisions and resolve these voices into a coherent and consistent narrative consciousness. But Roxana simply acts out the conflicts without perceiving their relationships to each other. For her, the split between the self who experiences and the self who relates those experiences is a necessary condition of existence and is certainly evidence of what John Richetti calls "the individualist dilemma." In this novel, however, these divisions also have a more specific provenance and hence a more explicit burden. Their provenance is the structure that Defoe's narrative transvestism lends to the novel, and their theme is the relationship of gender to narrative.

Thus Roxana's internal and pragmatic debate about the true nature of woman has its narrative echo in the Lady's frustrated attempts to relate her own history, and its structural origin in Defoe's imaginative creation of a female narrator whose gender and whose narrative he complicates by continual redefinition. The novel's own exploration of the instability of gendered categories makes clear that the goal of the transvestite narrative structure is not to create a "genuine" or believable woman but to investigate how the suggestive transgression of the categories of gender is a vehicle for the creation of a stable and expressive self.

Roxana has absorbed her society's rigid conception of gender roles, which declares that an independent woman is no woman at all. Although she makes sporadic attempts to redefine either herself or those gender roles so that she can be independent and yet remain a woman, simply by being a prostitute she has succumbed to patriarchy's valuation of woman as body rather than as voice. She may make her fortune off those men she characterizes as "Fools," but she also is dependent on them for her identity as well as for her livelihood. And when she is with a man, she goes into a kind of sleep or temporary retirement—effectively as mute and helpless as a tiny baby. Roxana can only narrate her own experience when she remains outside of it. When she is confronted with an experience from which she cannot maintain her distance, language (the male Relator's "clothes" or "performance") deserts her, and her narrative is silenced. She loses her voice when she finds a man to care for her and when her daughter Susan persists in her attempts to identify Roxana as her mother. Susan's pursuit finally silences Roxana because "her" narrative has been paradoxically enabled by the conception, which she has assimilated, of woman as silent body. Her collapse is dictated by the structural demands of narrative transvestism, whose ultimate goal is to enable the creative and interpretive task of the male author, not of the female narrator.[10]

[10]David Marshall, in *Figure of Theater,* says of Susan's pursuit of her mother: "the girl represents a reader who would not take Roxana at face value; such a reader

Clearly then, Defoe succeeds where Roxana fails. By moving the narrative self from the Lady to the Relator through the Writer to "I" and back again, he creates an ephemeral but effective "Man-Woman" who can both contain experience and articulate it. He establishes the boundaries between male and female and then engages the reader in a continual revision of those categories by thematizing the effect that transgressing those boundaries has on Roxana's attempts to create a self.

Early in her narrative, Roxana gives us an emphatic definition of the proper behavior for men and women:

> Never, Ladies, marry a Fool; any Husband rather than a Fool; with some other Husbands you may be unhappy, but with a Fool you will be miserable; . . . *nay,* be anything, be even an Old Maid, the worst of Nature's Curses, rather than take up with a Fool. (8)

It is no accident that Roxana defines both gender roles by telling us what men and woman should *not* be. This is the route she takes to creating a self: she is in search of an other against whom she can define her being. Her method is to define who she is by ruling out what she is not and who she is not like. This definition by opposition is characteristic of narrative transvestism. Here it takes the form of a negative injunction to the female reader: never marry a "Fool" (that is, a man who is naive about money), even if it means resigning yourself to being "the worst of Nature's Curses," an unmarried woman. It would not be so wrong to say that Roxana's efforts to follow her own advice motivate the rest of her adventures. She wants neither to marry a fool nor to be an old maid. That is, she refuses both of the definitions of woman that society offers her, and she comes to believe that she has to become a "Man-Woman" to exist outside those definitions. Very early in her narrative she voices the conventional wisdom that the locus of a woman's identity is her virtue: "without question, a Woman ought rather to die, than to prostitute her

---

would see too much, go too far—and therefore must be stopped" (152). This leads him to a very nice formulation about the effect of the novel's abrupt ending on the reader: "the reader, like the daughter, must be murdered" (153).

Virtue and Honour, let the Temptation be what it will" (29). By the time she has a fortune, whose disposition she needs to discuss with her financial advisor, she seems to have changed her mind:

> I knew no Reason the Men had to engross the whole Liberty of the Race, and make the Women, notwithstanding any disparity of Fortune, be subject to the Laws of Marriage, of their own making; that it was my Misfortune to be a Woman, but I was resolv'd it shou'd not be made worse by the Sex; and seeing Liberty seem'd to be the Men's Property, I wou'd be a *Man-Woman*; for as I was born free, I wou'd die so. (171)

But just two paragraphs later she emends this definition of herself: "with all this Wealth, I was yet a Whore, and was not averse to adding to my Estate at the farther Expence of my Virtue." She now values her fortune above her virtue, but she has agreed to the price: she has rented out her body to men and moved her self elsewhere. Roxana has turned the "Misfortune" of being a woman into a facsimile of the male's fortune (which she defines as "Liberty") by marketing the attribute that defines her to men as a woman: her body. In the process she effectively ceases to inhabit that body; she locates her identity in her fortune instead.

Roxana's body is valuable to her as a commodity rather than as the site of her being. Her careful bargaining with the Dutch merchant about whether or not they should marry is then really an exploration of what defines a woman. Roxana jealously guards her Man-Woman self (that is, her money) but freely gives her body. The Dutch merchant, assuming that with her body she has given him her self, is astonished to discover that she isn't accessible to him. Their negotiations eventually founder because, although he is offering protection and she is seeking it, he locates that vulnerable self who needs protection in her body, and she locates it in her money.

By the time they eventually do marry at the end of the book, the terms of Roxana's existence have changed: she feels the threat from Susan in her body, and being a financial Man-

Woman offers her no defense. But until then she abides by her
whore's creed of independence:

> I then did as good as confess . . . that tho' I cou'd give up my
> Virtue, and expose myself, yet I wou'd not give up my Money,
> which, tho' it was true, yet was really too gross for me to acknowl-
> edge, [. . . so] I gave it a new Turn, upon this Occasion, as
> follows:
> I told him . . . that I thought a Woman was a free Agent, as well
> as a Man, and was born free, and cou'd she manage herself suit-
> ably, might enjoy that Liberty to as much Purpose as the Men do;
> that a Woman gave herself entirely away from herself, in Mar-
> riage, . . . and the Woman was indeed, a meer Woman ever after,
> that is to say, a Slave. . . .
> He reply'd . . . that the Woman had nothing to do, but to eat the
> Fat, and drink the Sweet; to sit still, and look round her; be waited
> on, and made much of. . . .
> I return'd, that while a Woman was single, she was a Masculine
> in her politick Capacity; that she had then the full Command of
> what she had, and the full Direction of what she did; . . . and that
> if she gave away that Power, she merited to be as miserable as it
> was possible that any Creature cou'd be. (147–49)

Despite her resistance to marriage, and despite all of her di-
atribes against "Fools" and the state of servitude to which their
wives ("meer women" as she calls them) are reduced, Roxana
is entirely dependent upon men and upon male fantasies of
women for her livelihood and even for her identity. She works as
a whore long after she needs to, simply because she is not sure
she will continue to exist in any other capacity. She points this
out herself: "This, with some other Securities, made me a very
handsome Estate, of above a Thousand Pounds a Year; enough,
one wou'd think, to keep any Woman in *England* from being a
Whore" (164). Indeed, when Susan threatens to identify her as a
mother (rather than a whore, a Quaker, a Turkish "Roxana," or
any of her selves that depend for their existence upon merging
with an other), Roxana is terrified that she will not survive it; she
is convinced that acknowledging Susan will be her ruin. She
cannot be the other who lends definition to someone else.

Roxana's fear is that Susan will require of her what she requires of men: a container for her otherwise dispersed self. Since she herself is in need of such a container, she cannot provide one for her daughter. Moreover, she feels her own needs as predatory and so is terrified of being consumed by Susan's similar needs. Her refusal to marry the Dutch merchant is in part an effort to protect him and to preserve him as that clearly defined other in opposition to whom she can cobble together a provisional self. Predictably enough, she doesn't worry about corrupting or contaminating him through sex but through the mingling of their fortunes:

> I cannot omit what happen'd to me while all this was acting, tho' it was chearful Work in the main, yet I trembled every Joint of me, worse for ought I know, than ever *Belshazzer* did at the Handwriting on the Wall, and the Occasion was every way as just: *Unhappy Wretch,* said I to myself, *shall my ill-got Wealth, the Product of prosperous Lust, and of a vile and vicious Life of* Whoredom and Adultery, *be intermingled with the honest well-gotten Estate of this innocent Gentleman, to be a Moth and a Caterpillar among it, and bring the Judgements of Heaven upon him, and upon what he has, for my sake! Shall my Wickedness blast his Comforts. Shall I* be Fire in his Flax! *and be a Means to provoke Heaven to curse his Blessings!* God forbid! *I'll keep them asunder, if it be possible.* (259)

As so often occurs in this novel, the exchange or mingling of money carries an erotic charge and the concomitant risk of compromised integrity. And, because she locates her self in her fortune, Roxana applies the techniques she used to win her fortune to the creation of a self. She gains her temporary coherence and her ability to act in the world by a process remarkably like capital accumulation and expenditure: she hoards the parts of a provisional self that she gathers by temporarily merging with various men and with Amy, and then she expends it in her narrative.

But when she is successful at using men in this way, when she achieves that momentary independence, Roxana suffers agonies of conscience. At those times she adopts a deeply misogynistic voice, as she does in the passage cited above, to accuse herself of being a corrupting influence. Significantly, this voice identifies the site of her evil power as precisely that body she has done her best to disown. Consequently, it often seems to be the voice of patriarchy, or of the male Relator, intruding itself upon female experience, and for the reader it is as startling as a third-person interruption. The passage above, for example, comes in the midst of the "chearful work" of counting up the fortune her new husband has brought to their marriage.

In other instances, this moralizing voice seems equally disconnected from Roxana's behavior. But because these pronouncements seem like third-person interruptions of Roxana's monologue, they carry a certain abstract authority; because this voice is not obviously Roxana's, it seems to be objective. Just as Roxana is so often detached from her body and its experiences, these authoritative moralizing interruptions can serve to disconnect us from our experience of reading *Roxana*. Because Roxana's narrative offers us so many versions of her life and its moral content, we are tempted to grasp at the most clearly articulated of those versions simply to resolve the confusion. If we succumb to the temptation, then we are behaving like Roxana, like an incompletely formed character in a novel rather than like the readers of that novel.

Many critics have taken Defoe up on his offer of certainty; they agree with Roxana's seemingly objective evaluation of herself as a parasite or as an unnatural woman. She is called variously "the hard and calculating Roxana" and a woman who has a "frivolous and avaricious approach to life."[11] These, however, are only the verdicts of Roxana's intrusive, moralizing and self-condemning voice, and if we seize upon them, then we ignore the rest of her narrative and, in particular, that part of her experience and her character that is less easily categorized. Instead, our perspective as readers allows us to suspend judgment and to tolerate the contradictions in Roxana's story for long enough to see the more complicated pattern they form.

Defoe also presents us with a character (or, as I will explore

---

[11]The first phrase is from Moore, *Daniel Defoe*, p. 245. The second is from Paula Backscheider, *Daniel Defoe: Ambition and Innovation* (Lexington: University of Kentucky Press, 1986), p. 185.

later in this chapter, with an aspect of Roxana's character) in whom success in the world does not prompt agonies of conscience or the anxious reduction of experience to unexamined categories. Roxana's maid Amy is a happy pragmatist who never suffers from the split between body and self or experience and voice that so plagues her mistress. She is therefore also free of the bouts of indecision and passivity that so paralyze Roxana when she is unattached. And when Roxana is at her most passive, Amy urges her on to action or, failing that, acts or speaks for her.

Amy, while still perhaps an "unnatural" woman in the terms of Defoe's novel, is a highly effective character who cares for Roxana, manages her fortune, organizes Roxana's belated generosity to her children, and finally takes the brutal step she feels will free her mistress from the pursuing demon, her daughter Susan. For her the terms of existence are not complicated. From the very first she sees her way clear to caring for both herself and her mistress when Roxana's husband abandons her and they are thrust into the world of unmarried and unprotected women.

> O Madam, says *Amy*, I'd do any thing to get you out of this sad Condition; as to Honesty, I think Honesty is out of the Question, when Starving is the Case; are not we almost starv'd to Death? I am indeed, *said I*, and thou are for my sake; but to be a Whore, *Amy*! and there I stopt.
>
> Dear Madam, says *Amy*, if I will starve for your sake, I will be a Whore, or any thing, for your sake; why I would die for you, if I were put to it. (28)

Roxana worries about forfeiting her identity to the role of whore; Amy is more concerned with surviving than with being constrained by the world's definition of her. Roxana's dilemma defines her as a woman. Amy, who lacks this split between the body that experiences and the moralizing and interpretive voice that narrates those experiences, occupies a curious place in the gender hierarchy of the text. She often seems to be the complementary effective man to Roxana's passive woman, the other whose self-definition also outlines for Roxana the boundaries of her being. As the narrative progresses and as Amy becomes more complexly entwined in Roxana's financial and sexual dealings, she loses her female identity and gains more of a male one. She becomes an expert in financial matters. She stops flirting with Roxana's lovers, and she stops having lovers of her own.

The relationship between maid and mistress provides an arena for Defoe's exploration of gender and of the activities, the language, and the ways of being in the world that are available to men, to women, or to an unselfconsciously androgynous figure like Amy. The thematic issue of Roxana's struggle to become a Man-Woman who is free from, as Ian Watt puts it, "any involuntary involvement in the feminine role" (113), merges here with the structural issues raised by Defoe's narrative transvestism. For Roxana's pursuit of man's power and privilege in the world is, of course, the mirror image of Defoe's construction of a woman in whose clothes he can dress his fantasies and through whose voice he can speak of the constraints of gender. Defoe has created this dualistic world in which every aspect of existence presents itself as an impossible choice between mutually annihilating opposites. For him as well as for Roxana the construction of narrative presents itself as a choice between an enabling—if transforming—disguise and silence. And he, like his Man-Woman antiheroine, depends for his narrative effectiveness on an uneasy alliance of contradictory impulses.

Roxana's ultimate failure—the collapse into chaos of what had been the enabling tension between herself, Amy, and Susan—is equally dictated by the structure of narrative transvestism: successful transvestism never achieves stability in one gender role or the other. Rather, it creates an ephemeral third gender which is not limited to either the male or female role but which has access to both. Through a process of continual negation the transvestite self endlessly makes and unmakes an identity. This not-woman not-man exists in the brief moments of stasis—the breaths, as it were—between negations, when the two contradictory impulses (away from woman and away from man) coexist in creative disharmony.

Susan's attempts to get Roxana to acknowledge her as a

daughter precipitate a crisis because such an acknowledgment would force Roxana (and by extension Defoe) to live with the limitations of the woman's role. But Roxana exists by virtue of being undefined. She absorbs and then rejects aspects of character from Amy and from her succession of lovers in response to demands or threats from the world. Like the transvestite, she achieves a kind of immortality in this way: although she makes an occasional (and usually chronologically inconsistent) reference to her age, Roxana is forever young and beautiful, and forever fertile.

Defoe's use of a woman's voice and his own authorial cycle of merging with and then distancing himself from what he defines as the feminine characteristics of that voice give an existential cast to the otherwise merely titillating play between Amy, Roxana, and Roxana's male lovers in bed. When Roxana sends Amy to bed with the landlord in her stead she is trying to define Amy as a woman in the same way that she—in the moralizing parts of her narrative—defines herself. And when the rich lord questions whether or not Amy is truly the woman she has appeared to be, he is clearly trying to use her to define himself as a man. In this world the search for a self is a competition for scarce resources; what others are you cannot be, and the space they take up defines the space you can inhabit.

At the very beginning of their life together, when she and Amy are not as fully merged as they will later be, Roxana feels compelled to substitute Amy for herself in bed with the landlord for whom she first turns whore so that "my Maid should be a Whore too, and should not reproach me with it" (47). Amy has already identified herself as Roxana's protector or mother, but she also engages in bawdy bantering with the landlord, with whom she jests that "she would let him lye with her, if he would but be kinder to [Roxana]" (44), and she is still in competition with Roxana over who is the most womanly of the two. She teases her about not yet being pregnant by the landlord: "Law, Madam, says Amy, what have you been doing? . . . Master wou'd have got me with-Child twice in that time" (45).

But by the time Roxana and Amy are being kept in luxury by a rich lord, Amy is no longer competing with Roxana for the badge of womanliness. By this point in the narrative we no longer hear about her own lovers or her own abandoned children. She is Roxana's silently efficient manager who lives vicariously through Roxana's adventures even as she provides a protective container for Roxana's own unstable identity. Thus the relationship between the two has become considerably more complex; it is often difficult to tell whether Amy and Roxana are functioning as one being or two. Roxana's account of the evening's confusion reveals a curious combination of advocacy and detached bemusement.

It happen'd pleasantly enough one Night; his Lordship had staid late, and I not expecting him that Night, had taken *Amy* to-Bed with me, and when my Lord came into the Chamber, we were both fast asleep. . . .

Amy was frighted out of her Wits, and cry'd out; *I said calmly*, indeed my Lord, I did not expect you to-Night, and we have been a little frighted to-Night with Fire: O! says he, I see you have got a Bedfellow with you; I began to make an Apology, No, no, says my Lord, you need no Excuse, 'tis not a Man-Bedfellow I see; but then talking merrily enough, he catch'd his Words back; but hark-ye, says he, now I think on't, how shall I be satisfied it is not a Man-Bedfellow? O, says I, I dare say your Lordship is satisfy'd 'tis poor Amy; yes, says he, 'tis Mrs. *Amy*, but how do I know what *Amy* is? It may be Mr. *Amy*, for ought I know; I hope you'll give me Leave to be satisfy'd: I told him, Yes, by all means I wou'd have his Lordship satisfy'd, but I suppos'd he knew who she was.

Well, he fell foul of poor *Amy*, and indeed, I thought once he wou'd have carry'd the Jest on before my Face, as was once done in a like Case; but his Lordship was not so hot neither; but he wou'd know whether *Amy* was Mr. *Amy*, or Mrs. *Amy*, and so I suppose he did; and then being satisfy'd in that doubtful Case, he walk'd to the farther-end of the Room, and went into a little Closet, and sat down. (186–87)

It is worth tracing the circuitous route of Roxana's narrative through this curious episode. It begins with Roxana in bed with

Amy, a seemingly acceptable substitute for the absent lord. When the lord comes in on them, Amy is terrified (for reasons we are left to conjecture about) and Roxana is apologetic about her "Bedfellow." The apology leads the lord to wonder, apparently for the first time, how to know "what *Amy* is." He had had intercourse with Roxana and so knows her to be a woman—that is, a being defined by her body. But he has never tested Amy in this way, and so, "it may be Mr. *Amy,* for ought I know."

Amy is not amused by the lord's suggestion that he be "satisfy'd" that she is a woman, and unlike that earlier occasion on which she set out to make Amy a woman, Roxana has no interest in pushing either of them to action. That earlier time, Roxana assumed that if Amy had sex with the landlord, then she would become (or be revealed as) a corrupting influence like Roxana herself, and a creature of similarly ill-defined boundaries. This time, however, she no longer needs such "satisfaction" about Amy's sexual identity. Instead, she rather dryly notes that his Lordship is not man enough to make a woman of Amy: "but his Lordship was not so hot neither."

In the novel's terms, no man can make a woman of Amy because she doesn't define herself by opposition the way Roxana does and as Defoe does through Roxana. For Roxana, sex with a man defines the space that she as a woman can inhabit. That space turns out to be the physical limits of her woman's body. But Amy is not engaged in this transvestite process and truly, *may* be Mr. Amy.

From this impasse the episode can only end in anticlimax. The lord insists on knowing "whether *Amy* was Mr. *Amy* or Mrs. *Amy,*" and Roxana "suppose[s]" he found out, but she only recounts his giving up and wandering off. The "doubtful Case" is never really resolved; the lord goes "into a little Closet, and [sits] down." Amy returns to her maid's role and makes up a bed for the lord, and the three of them go on as before.

Through much of this chapter I have written of Roxana's needs and fears and of her relationship to Amy. But of course "Roxana" is a literary construct, and "her" needs and fears are aspects of Defoe's own creative process, which, like hers, is one of self-definition through negation. Defoe has indeed created a narrator who is limited in ways that are useful to him. But Roxana's limitations are not necessarily Defoe's limitations; he is as much Amy and Susan and the Dutch merchant and Roxana's first husband as he is Roxana herself. Each of these characters plays a part in the dynamic of narrative transvestism, and the structural demands of that transvestism determine the thematic exploration of the creation of a self.

Roxana is, for example, deeply ambivalent about being a woman. But of course she is not a woman; she is Defoe's other, a construct which allows him to complete himself and so to express that self in narrative. Thus her ambivalence is his narrative device and a gamble that affects the way we read the novel.

By creating a woman who is so determined to exist outside of conventional gender categories, Defoe risks irreparably fragmenting his narrator to gain his readers' participation in her (and his) quest. And Roxana does become more fragmented in the course of the novel. Aspects of her character that conflict with each other in the early part of her narrative get dispersed to other figures in the text by its end. As Defoe's plot exerts pressure on those points of contradiction, Roxana, Amy, and Susan begin to function almost as a single consciousness. In an elaborate mirroring of her preoccupation with the accumulation and spending of capital, Roxana gathers and then disperses aspects of the narrative self and the compulsions that drive that narrative. The boundaries between the three women become less and less distinct until Defoe has a tripartite female narrative self with which to work out the cycle of transvestite creation, which eventually becomes so complicated that it takes three women (Amy, Susan, and Roxana) to make one man (the Relator, or Defoe).

The Accumulation and Squandering
of the Self: Amy, Susan, and Roxana

Despite her concerted efforts to become independent (and independently wealthy), Roxana is essentially a passive creature

of a helplessly chameleon nature. She becomes whatever circumstances, Amy, or any rich gentleman demands of her. It is as
if, when she is unattached, or unmirrored, she ceases to exit. She
is only defined for us as the reflection of someone else's desires;
she has to dissemble or masquerade in order to exist at all. In the
course of her narrative she (or more accurately, her body) is
revealed as remarkably protean and for the most part ageless.
And because her disguises are so effective, they call into question the sharp division between the mask and the undisguised
self. For example, when Roxana wants to start a new life (because, as she tells Amy, she doesn't want her children to find
that "their Mother, however rich she may be, is at best but a
Whore" [208]), she simply moves to another part of town and
acquires the clothing and mannerisms of a Quaker:

> Says *Amy*, I guess your Meaning; it is a perfect Disguise to you;
> why you look quite another-body, I should not have known you
> myself; nay, says *Amy*, more than that, it makes you look ten Years
> younger than you did.
>   Nothing could please me better than that; . . . and there was not
> a QUAKER in the Town look'd less like a Counterfeit than I did.
> (211–13)

Coming from Amy, who has cared for the helpless infant in
Roxana for years, the statement "I should not have known you
myself" is a powerful one. It is particularly resonant in this
context because Roxana's unacknowledged reason for moving is
to fool her daughter Susan, who has come dangerously close to
identifying the "turkish Roxana" as her mother. Not only does
Roxana's metamorphosis into a Quaker make her appear too
morally correct to have ever been a whore, but it makes her look
"ten Years younger," that is, ten years too young to have a
daughter Susan's age.

This masquerade, like most of Roxana's other roles, is pre-
ceded by a period of morose passivity and precipitated by a
flurry of activity on Amy's part. (Amy finds the house and the
Quaker landlady; Roxana takes on the protective coloration of

her surroundings.) And Roxana is as truly a Quaker as she ever was a whore, a royal mistress, or a successful capitalist; "there was not a QUAKER in the Town look'd less like a Counterfeit than I did." She is not a counterfeit as a Quaker because her entire being is a masquerade.

Defoe has constructed a female narrator for whom the source of all being is masquerade because she allows him to re-create on the level of theme the anxieties of self-creation. Once having recreated that dilemma in the fictional realm, Defoe as author has access to solutions that Roxana (or Defoe when he is not an author) never sees. Most obviously, he is not paralyzed between two unacceptable extremes as is Roxana. Through the device of narrative transvestism he has access to that Man-Woman state to which she so aspires.

All of the conflicts and internal contradictions that immobilize Roxana and make her (in the eyes of many critics) an insufficiently developed character are, in fact, the traces of Defoe's complex transvestite narrative. On every conceivable level of his text he sets up binary oppositions and then exploits the creative tension between them. His authorial distance allows him access to each role while protecting him from the limits of any of them. Roxana is finally defined and so trapped by her woman's body. She is Susan's mother, and this fact determines her fate even after Amy has destroyed the evidence of motherhood by murdering Susan. But Defoe remains safely in the realm of language—uncontaminated by birth and so not subject to death. In a letter to Robert Harley, Defoe revealed just how aware he was that the endless process (and not its constituent parts) was the source of his power as an author: "With the Glasgow Mutineers I am to be a fish Merchant, with the Aberdeen Men a woollen and with the Perth and Western men a Linen Manufacturer, and still at the End of all Discourse the Union is the Essentiall and I am all to Every one that I may Gain some."[12] It is equally the union

[12]G. H. Healey, ed., *The Letters of Daniel Defoe* (Oxford: Oxford University Press, 1955), p. 43, cited in Richetti, *Defoe's Narratives*, p. 1. The letter is dated 26 November 1706.

between Roxana, Amy, and Susan that is essential, and by shifting the active self between them in his narrative, Defoe is "all to
Every one that [he] may Gain some."

Susan is Roxana's oldest child, the first of the five legitimate
children her husband leaves her with (the getting of children
being, as she puts it, "the only Work (perhaps) that Fools are
good for" [10]) when he abandons her. Roxana is, of course,
paralyzed by her misery at this abandonment, but Amy arranges
to have most of the children taken in by their father's relatives.
Susan, who was about six years old when she was left on her
uncle's doorstep, eventually turns up as a maid in Roxana's own
house. During her employment there, she only sees her mistress
in her Turkish guise and so doesn't connect her with the mother
she is so desperately seeking. Roxana, for her part, is determined to keep things that way: "I cou'd by no means think of
ever letting the Children know what a kind of Creature they
ow'd their Being to, or giving them an Occasion to upbraid their
Mother with her scandalous Life" (205). But of course Susan
doesn't owe her being to the whore Roxana has become but to
the legitimate wife and mother she was. Indeed, Roxana's mortal fear of being discovered by Susan is entirely out of proportion
to what the actual consequences of such a discovery might be.
The last third of the book is occupied with Susan's pursuit and
Roxana's flight, but it is never entirely clear whether Roxana is
fleeing Susan's identification of her or her own passionate identification with her daughter. For Susan is, as Roxana tells us
rather belatedly, "my own Name" (205). "Roxana" is a name, or
rather an epithet, she has acquired from one of her most effective
disguises: "At the finishing the Dance, . . . one of the Gentlemen cry'd out, *Roxana! Roxana!* by—, with an Oath, upon which
foolish Accident I had the Name of *Roxana* presently fix'd upon
me . . . as effectually as if I had been Christen'd *Roxana*: . . . and
so the Name *Roxana* was the Toast at, and about the Court" (176).
This is the same public dance that Susan saw when she was a
servant in Roxana's household, making her, curiously enough, a
spectator at her mother's birth and christening.

In the fluctuating dyads that Roxana, Amy, and Susan form, Roxana is never a mother but always a helpless infant. Amy cares for her and on her behalf for Susan, who logically enough concludes that Amy is her real mother.

> And then she calls Amy her *Dear Mother*, and hung about her Neck again, crying still vehemently. This last Part of the Girl's Words alarm'd *Amy*, and, *as she told me*, frighted her terribly; nay, she was so confounded with it, that she was not able to govern herself, or to conceal her Disorder from the Girl herself, *as you shall hear*: Amy was at a full Stop, and confus'd to the last Degree, and the Girl a sharp Jade, turn'd it upon her: My dear Mother, *says she*, do not be uneasie about it; I know it all; but do not be uneasie, I won't let my sister know a word of it, or my Brother either, without you give me leave; but don't disown me now you have found me; don't hide yourself from me any longer; I can't bear that, *says she*, it will break my Heart.
> I think the Girl's mad, *says Amy*. (267)

In fact, it is precisely Susan's demand that Roxana behave like a mother that so terrifies her. She has never acted the part of a mother or even made herself known to any of the countless children she's had since those first five. Of a child she has by the Dutch merchant she says: "I did not love the Child nor love to see it; and tho' I had provided for it, yet I did it by *Amy's* Hand, and had not seen it above twice in four Years; being privately resolv'd that when it grew up it shou'd not be able to call me Mother" (228).

Typically enough, she refers to the child as "it." Similarly, she often denies Susan her own name, calling her, instead, a "Jade," a "Slut," or "the Girl." She is strikingly lacking in empathy for Susan and the pain her desperate search for an identity has brought her. She is incapable of compassion because Susan is demanding of her precisely what Roxana herself so desperately needs: a mirror that might reflect a coherent self. At various times Roxana finds a temporarily reassuring mirror in Amy, in a man, or in her hoard of money, but Susan threatens to sever the fragile arrangements by which Roxana secures such an ephemeral self. Roxana first says she's afraid that acknowledging Susan will constrain her from her activity as a whore, and then that it would destroy her marriage to the merchant. Her behavior reveals that she's most worried about losing Amy's mothering ministrations, which she might transfer to Susan. Losing Amy would, of course, be losing the part of her self that functions in the world.

In their response to the threat Susan presents, Roxana and Amy act as if they were parts of one psyche. Even Roxana can't tell where the boundary lies between her own thoughts and Amy's: "I must acknowledge, the Notion of being discover'd, carried with it so many frightful *Ideas,* and hurry'd my Thoughts so much, that I was scarce myself, any more than *Amy*" (273). The syntax of this "acknowledgment" is confusing in the extreme. Is Roxana scarce herself any more than she's Amy? Is Amy no more Roxana than Roxana is? Or is Amy so affected by Roxana's dilemma that she is, like Roxana, scarce herself? Amy takes on Roxana's cause and her fears as if they were her own. And eventually she acts on the wishes that Roxana most vehemently denies.

> But this, [Susan taking Amy for her mother] did not disquiet me half so much, as that the young Slut had got the Name of *Roxana* by the end; . . . *Amy* was so provok'd, that she told me, *in short,* she began to think it wou'd be absolutely necessary to murther her: That Expression fill'd me with Horror; all my Blood ran chill in my Veins, and a Fit of trembling seiz'd me, that I cou'd not speak a good-while; at last, What is the Devil in you, *Amy, said I?* Nay, nay, *says she,* let it be the Devil, or not the Devil, if I thought she know one tittle of your History, I wou'd dispatch her if she were my own Daughter a thousand times; and I *says I in a Rage,* as well as I love you, wou'd be the first that shou'd put the Halter about your Neck. (270–71)

Roxana has already wished Susan dead, but she has also had such a passionate response to her that Susan is necessary to her being just as is Amy. In fact, Roxana's response to Susan is unlike any other response she recounts in her narrative. Roxana, whose body has all along been a mere container—a kind of transvestite way station for Defoe and a marketable commodity for his narrator—has an uncontrollable physical response to her daughter's presence.

> I cannot but take Notice here, that notwithstanding there was a secret Horror upon my Mind, and I was ready to sink when I came close to her, to salute her; yet it was a secret inconceivable Pleasure to me when I kiss'd her, to know that I kiss'd my own Child; my own Flesh and Blood, born of my Body; and who I had never kiss'd since I took that fatal Farewell of them all, with a Million of Tears, and a Heart almost dead with Grief, when *Amy* and the Good woman took them all away, and went with them to *Spittle-Fields*: No Pen can describe, no words can express, *I say*, the strange Impression which this thing made upon my Spirits; I felt something shoot thro' my Blood; my Heart flutter'd; my Head flash'd, and was dizzy, and all within me *as I thought*, turn'd about, and much ado I had, not to abandon myself to an Excess of Passion at the first Sight of her, much more when my Lips touch'd her Face; I thought I must have taken her in my Arms, and kiss'd her again a thousand times, whether I wou'd or no.
>   But I rous'd up my Judgment, and shook it off. (277)

When she sees Susan, words are inadequate to express her feelings. On other occasions, Susan renders her speechless. On this occasion, she makes the ambiguous statement that "No Pen can describe, no words can express, *I say*, the strange Impression which this thing made upon my Spirits." The emphatic "*I say*" asserts the power of direct speech even while Roxana claims that her feelings cannot be conveyed in words. And, of course, Roxana's claim is Defoe's admission: the "Pen" that cannot describe her experience is his. Thus Defoe reveals the impulses that govern narrative transvestism. A woman—even one of his own making—has access to experience that is denied to him. By temporarily adopting her voice, he gains partial access to that experience while retaining the control over language and abstraction that is denied to women. He admits that access is only partial (there may even be defects in his performance), but total access would require being trapped as Roxana so clearly is. As the transvestite narrator, Defoe can be articulate about the inadequacy of language to express bodily experience rather than being rendered mute by that experience.

There is, however, another twist to this borrowing of perspectives. The definition of woman as inexpressive body is Defoe's own (although it is, of course, governed and supported by a cultural norm); he needs to keep woman's being narrowly defined in order to define himself effectively against it. Roxana operates in a similar manner when she declares that men are "Fools" and women are either "meer Wives" or "Whores."

It is no accident then that Roxana—who all along has defined herself as a Man-Woman who situates her being in her fortune and not in her body—is finally "brought low" by the inescapable biological fact of motherhood. And when she loses her status as an independent Man-Woman, she loses her effectiveness, her speech, and eventually her existence. These are the limitations to his female narrator that enable Defoe's text.

Roxana recognizes Susan as she has never recognized herself. Susan is not the Man-Woman that Roxana has aspired to be or that Mr./Mrs. Amy effectively is. For her the problem of identity is not one of gender but of parentage. Unlike Roxana, who is passive and silent until she can borrow a self from a man to whom she is attached, Susan's astounding, clever, unstoppable "Discourse" knows no barriers. While Roxana is a mere body and therefore substantially changed by a costume or by the expectations of her companions, Susan exists in the paradoxically more substantial realm of emotion and imagination. Even after Amy has murdered her, Susan's being remains intact, and her presence is heightened by her physical absence: "As for the poor Girl herself, she was ever before my Eyes; I saw her by-Night, and by-Day; she haunted my Imagination, if she did not haunt the House; my Fancy show'd her me in a hundred Shapes and Postures; sleeping or waking she was with me" (325).

This powerful image speaks of a passionate connection between mother and daughter that is equalled in the novel only by Roxana's dependence on Amy, of whom Roxana says: "But, *as I said*, Amy effected all afterwards, without my Knowledge, for which I gave her my hearty Curse, tho' I cou'd do little more; for to have fall'n upon *Amy*, had been to have murther'd myself: But this Tragedy requires a longer Story than I have room for here: *I return to my Journey* (302).

Like Roxana's account of the grief she feels and of how she is still haunted by Susan's image, this statement of anger at Amy is most remarkable for what it leaves out. Roxana never explains to us why she has such a powerful attachment to this daughter she hardly knows. She similarly tosses off the assertion that she can take no action against Amy because "to have fall'n upon *Amy*, had been to have murther'd myself." Instead, she returns to her story, as if these were simply digressions like any other of the thousand unimportant digressions. We are left to conjecture about what might have prompted such passions and about what might be the connection between Roxana's feelings and her behavior.

In fact, there is an enormous gap in the entire presentation of Susan's story: nothing in the plot demands Susan's murder. Roxana believes that her daughter is out to destroy her and is waiting "till she might perhaps, do it more to my Disadvantage" (281), but Susan has no real power over her life.[13] Her demand that Roxana acknowledge her (a not unreasonable demand for a child to make of a mother) simply carries with it the unspecified threat of exposure. The threat is unspecified because it can have no impact on the level of plot: Roxana is rich enough and safe enough in her new marriage. Rather, the threat is metaphorical and structural. The metaphorical threat is that Roxana's masquerades would be shown to be masquerades; her Man-Woman self (that is, in the novel's terms, her complete and functioning self) would be revealed as a fragile construct, and she would be left exposed as an inexpressive body, a mere woman. On the

---

[13]Roxana is terrified that her new husband will find out about these children from her past and about her ill-treatment of them, but Susan is the child of a legitimate marriage, and Amy took more care to see they were well situated than did she or Roxana for any of the later children.

structural level, the threat is to Defoe's narrative. Susan does not fall into either one of the opposing gender categories Defoe shuttles between in the process that has produced the novel. Rather, she is the emblem of a powerful and uncontrollable femininity whose voice cannot be resolved into his. She is crucial to the novel; Roxana's unreasoning fear of and attraction to Susan mirror the fear and envy that prompted Defoe to appropriate a woman's voice in the first place. But she also threatens the creative structure he has worked out; the female persona that allows Defoe to express mastery over his own creative dilemma also threatens to pollute or subvert that mastery. The novel's structure—rather than its plot—thus demands that Susan be killed. And once she is murdered, Amy and Roxana return to their former relationship in which the two women combine to make one effective being—in the novel's terms, a man.

Even when her rage and despair has been caused by Amy's murder of Susan, Roxana needs Amy (her active and masculine half) if she is to be able to express that despair:

> I was struck as with a Blast from Heaven, at the reading her Letter; I fell into a Fit of trembling, from Head to Foot; and I ran raving about the Room like a Mad-Woman; I had nobody [because Amy's not there] to speak a Word to, to give Vent to my Passion; nor did I speak a Word for a good-while, till after it had almost overcome me: I threw myself on the Bed, and cry'd out, *Lord be merciful to me, she has murther'd my Child*, and with that, a Flood of Tears burst out, and I cry'd vehemently for above an Hour. (323)

From here Roxana's narrative, which has been so anchored in concrete details and specific situations, wanders into the vague realm of the abstract. Roxana can't tell us if Susan was really murdered or if Amy really murdered her. She suffers from a confused notion of avenging fate, but she is not sure if her misery and repentance for this crime that might have been is genuine or only (as she calls it on another occasion) a "Storm-Repentance." Amy, who has been banished, mysteriously reappears in her life, but "I can say no more now" (329) Roxana tells us, and her narrative trails off.

Roxana ends essentially as it began. Roxana's narrative is divided against itself, and she has reembarked on her flight from identity to identity, abandoning each one as she begins to feel trapped within it. *Roxana* reveals this cycle in concrete terms: when its heroine successfully accumulates character from those around her, she acquires capital, and the interest on that capital is her narrative. When her relationships with others become unprofitable (as they necessarily do), she loses her fortune and retreats into silence. But Roxana's instability is on another level a mirroring of Defoe's creative process: she is a wealthy, independent and articulate Man-Woman when he needs an other into which he can imaginatively project his voice. When he is ready to return to his newly reaffirmed self before embarking on the process again, he withdraws from his creation and Roxana falls silent.

At the height of her financial success, and just about the time Susan begins to plague her, Roxana feels a compulsion to question the profession that at other times she claims has freed her: "and it came so very strong upon my Mind one Morning, when I had been lying some time in my Bed, as if somebody had ask'd me the Question, *What was I a Whore for now?*" (200–201).

She mocks her own answer, which is that she's honoring her arrangement with the "wicked old Lord" who is keeping her. In the midst of this debate with herself, Roxana quotes Defoe, "For HONESTY and HONOUR, are the same,"[14] to show that she can never be free of the corruption that marks her as a woman: "I was indeed, too fast held for any Reasoning that I was then Mistress of, to deliver me" (202).

This is however the moment at which she decides to seek out the five children she abandoned at the beginning of her tale, and to provide for them as best she can. Defoe thus exploits the irony of his own position as Roxana's creator as well as her position as

[14]The Oxford paperback edition (ed. Jane Jack) identifies this as "almost certainly a line of Defoe's own" (332). The Penguin edition (1982, ed. David Blewett) gives a more concrete reference in n. 222 (p. 396), citing the exact line from Defoe's "The Character of the Late Dr. Samuel Annesley" (1697), in *A True Collection of the Writings of the Author of the True Born Englishman* (1703), p. 113.

a mere enabling construction for a male author. She is his construction, and he can have her cite his other writings as a source of moral authority, but she is only useful to him if she is genuinely other and if in speaking his words she also alters them.

Defoe's words thus become the utterances of a "Man-Woman," a hybrid creature who is both himself and not himself. The paradoxical and unstable existence to which he has condemned Roxana is, of course, also the mirror of his authorial method. By acknowledging this fact, Defoe draws us further into the text so that we are reading two stories at once: Roxana's history and the authorial story of creation. We cannot help but be engaged with both, and the continual shifts in perspective that the different stories require of us heighten the intensity of the reading experience and make of that experience another object lesson: to read this transvestite narrative, we must become something like transvestite readers. But rather than men temporarily dressing as women, we are readers temporarily assuming the prerogatives of authors. As readers we willingly suspend our knowledge that this narrative and these characters are fictional, yet like authors we also participate in their construction. We read Roxana's story as her own, yet we share the authorial perspective that allows us to make of that story the coherent history that she never experiences. And it becomes increasingly difficult to separate the reader from the author in ourselves. Like Defoe, who can explore but not escape the paradoxes of his transvestite narrative, in reading *Roxana* we learn to exploit the continual interchange between the two identities.

3
Richardson and *Clarissa:*
The Author as Reader

Writing is an act of self-display and as such an invitation to mockery—or at the very least, to criticism. Every writer feels this vulnerability, no matter how grandiose a vision of the self and the work she or he conjures up. Indeed, as every critic as well as every novelist knows, a great deal of the hard work of writing comes from the effort to construct a carapace over the vulnerable self without dimming the dazzle of the display of that self. This carapace may take the form of learned research or of masterful exploitation of a complicated poetic form or of oracular pronouncements that never deign to explain themselves. In one way or another, each of us constructs a writing self who can achieve the tricky balance between self-expression and self-defense.

Much enduring literature is characterized by a certain slippery suggestiveness about authorial control of or subjection to the fictional narrator. Much of our involvement and delight as readers stems from our attempts to know this author both through and around the characters she or he presents to us. We are enticed by the secrets the author deliberately seems to reveal, and captivated by the unforeseen connections the work offers but the author perhaps never fully sees.

It is all the more striking then that Samuel Richardson, who presents us with an elaborate series of nested writing selves and who is clearly an adept at the dance of revealing self-concealment, has traditionally been portrayed as a man who wrote his novels—and in particular the astonishingly rich and powerful *Clarissa*—almost in spite of himself. Displaying a common (and as I will show, highly significant) tendency to equate Richardson's fiction with his life, critics have added the author's coy disingenuousness in his personal correspondence to Pamela Andrews's unconvincing sexual innocence and Clarissa Harlowe's denial of her attraction to Lovelace to buttress their claim that Richardson didn't know himself well enough to have any idea what he was doing in his novels.[1]

Not by accident, all of these examples have to do with sex. As Fielding's parody *Shamela* shows, it doesn't take a post-Freudian mind to search for hypocrisy or contradictions in the realm of sexual desire. And, of course, Clarissa's and Lovelace's own ignorance of the nature of their sexual desires and of the role that ignorance plays in the plot of *Clarissa* make the topic of sex crucial to any reading of their characters. Furthermore, a concern with sexuality and gender and the impact of each of them on writing is deeply embedded in the structure of *Clarissa*. As I show in this chapter's third section, Richardson's use of narrative transvestism makes the thematization of the status of the body and its ambiguous desires practically inevitable. One cannot adopt the voice of an other whose difference is primarily defined by the body without reflecting that bodily difference in the metaphorical body of the text. The structures of narrative transvestism and the epistolary novel also enable these issues to be thematized in *Clarissa* without, perhaps, being fully understood by Richardson. And, as we will see, Richardson typically

[1]Perhaps the most striking example of this kind of analysis of the novels through an investigation of Richardson's sexual biography is to be found in Dorothy Van Ghent's criticism of *Clarissa* in *The English Novel: Form and Function* (New York: Rinehart, 1953), but one can find evidence of Richardson's being dismissed as a novelist because he was a prude in any number of critical works. In particular, critics have mocked Pamela's pious but inflaming sexual innocence and the fact that the heroine of *Clarissa* can be said (if one views the plot in the crudest terms) to have died from sexual intercourse.

knows and doesn't know the importance of what he writes. His method itself is paradoxical: he produces his narrative by silencing his own voice.

Even his model letters for the up-and-coming middle class, *Familiar Letters Written on Important Occasions,* reveal a remarkably chameleon-like authorial persona. Meant to inculcate a moral and social as well as a rhetorical code, the letters display in astonishing variety and fluency Richardson's talent for projecting himself into the assumptions, desires, and concrete details of an imaginary other's life. Over and over again Richardson finds his narrative voice in the most unlikely fictional bodies—in the gaps, as it were, between the formal constraints of any genre; in the differences, that is, between his experience of life and the lives he imagines for his letter writers. The epistolary form allows him to parcel out his contradictions among his various letter writers. It also allows him to enact the cycles of narrative transvestism without destabilizing his narrative as Defoe did in *Roxana.* Far from weakening the text, those contradictory impulses give it richness and energy, something Richardson himself recognized:

> The undecided Events [in *Clarissa*] are sufficiently pointed out to the Reader, to whom in this Sort of Writing, something, as I have hinted, should be left to make out or debate upon. The whole Story abounds with Situations and Circumstances debatable. It is not an unartful Management to interest the Readers so much in the Story, as to make them differ in Opinion as to the Capital Articles, and by Leading one, to espouse one, another, another, Opinion, make them all, if not Authors, Carpers.[2]

Richardson's stated moral purpose for *Clarissa,* for example, "to caution parents against the undue exertion of their natural authority over their children in the great article of marriage: and children against preferring a man of pleasure to a man of probity,

---

[2]*The Selected Letters of Samuel Richardson,* ed. John Carroll (Oxford: Clarendon Press, 1964), p. 296. Future pages will be in parentheses in the text. All emphases are Richardson's.

upon that dangerous but too commonly received notion, *that a reformed rake makes the best husband,"*[3] does not even hint at the rich complexity and ambiguity of the novel itself. Some of the richness of the fiction, however, stems precisely from the disjunction between Richardson's didactic pronouncements and the morally ambiguous universe his characters create through their letters. As readers we attempt to fill this interpretive gap in the text. Thus we come to inhabit Richardson's fictional world, to lend our imaginations and our passions to this cooperative venture. And Richardson makes it amply clear in his personal correspondence that he knew that the seeming absence of an author drew his readers into his novel. This is not so much to say that he deliberately absented himself in order to entice his readers into his texts, but that he found a way to use the limitations of the structures that came naturally to him.

Again and again we see him deliberately tapping the power of the fictional world he could create but not control. He claims the credit for his novels at the same time as he denies responsibility for his characters' behavior. He hasn't created these characters, he asserts, but he knows them very well. Anyone searching for the "true author" of these texts must look elsewhere. And if we follow Richardson's pointers, that "elsewhere" always turns out to be wherever Richardson is not. He refers us to some nameless authority that propels these texts (by turns the absent letter writer, the omniscient editor, and the assumed reader), and he acknowledges or disavows each position as his own as it becomes convenient for him.

Richardson is everywhere and nowhere in his texts, and this makes him impossible to pin down. Thus situated he can, for example, as a reader of his own text, remain genuinely artless in his admiration for his heroine while as an author he is astutely aware of the uses of that same kind of artlessness with which he has endowed his artful creation, Clarissa. And he quite deliber-

[3]Samuel Richardson, *Clarissa, or the History of a Young Lady,* ed. Angus Ross (New York: Penguin, 1985), p. 36.

ately fosters this same willing and marginally self-aware suspension of disbelief in his readers:

> Will you, good Sir, allow me to mention, that I could wish that the
> *Air* of Genuineness had been kept up, tho' I want not the letters to
> be *thought* genuine; only so far kept up, I mean, as that they should
> not prefatically be owned *not* to be genuine: and this for fear of
> weakening their Influence where any of them are aimed to be
> exemplary; as well as to avoid hurting that kind of Historical Faith
> which Fiction itself is generally read with, tho' we know it to be
> Fiction. (Carroll 85)

Richardson's half-belief in his own fictions is perhaps not so different from the balance between active creation of and complete absorption in his or her fictional world achieved by any good novelist. It is, however, quite different from the traditional critical view of Richardson as an accidental novelist. I don't intend to claim that Richardson was wholly conscious of the effect of every word or every structural device in Clarissa. I seek instead to show that, as his personal letters tell us again and again, Richardson acknowledged and acquiesced to the strange felicity of his letter writing; he trusted his characters more than himself.

This stance makes for what one might call in Bakhtin's terms the dialogic quality of *Clarissa*.[4] For example, Clarissa denies her attraction to Lovelace; Anna Howe perceives it and taxes her friend with hypocrisy; Lovelace exploits it and mistakes it for moral weakness; and Richardson allows Clarissa's attraction to be central to the plot but tries to make it irrelevant to the moral message in his novel. This insistence on the clear moral message

---

[4]M. M. Bakhtin, *The Dialogic Imagination*. The idea of the dialogic, while useful, doesn't place sufficient emphasis on the position of the author within the narrative structure of the novel. It also tends to obscure the hierarchy of voices in this novel (which is, after all, Clarissa's book in spite of Lovelace's protean and prolific letter writing) and the thematization of the problem of writing that is not read and voices that are not heard. Most of all, the idea of the dialogic obscures the issue of gender and of the transgression of gender boundaries. For more on this topic, see the third section of this chapter.

of his text is one of many ways in which "Richardson" tried (and failed) to reassert control over "the others." As I will detail later, he fails to define an absolute and incontrovertible interpretation for his novel, but his attempts become part of a richly complicated lesson in reading that is not so unlike what he set out to do. He was, for example, deeply offended when *Clarissa*'s readers, noting that she refused to acknowledge what her behavior betrayed—that she found Lovelace powerfully attractive—taxed his heroine with hypocrisy. Richardson himself found Lovelace attractive, but that doesn't stop him from condemning the women readers who felt the same way. Tellingly, Richardson's solution was not to make Clarissa more self-aware but to make Lovelace less attractive.[5] This solution implies that Richardson made an interesting psychological assumption about his readers: that they (particularly the susceptible females) found Lovelace attractive and were projecting their own feelings onto Clarissa. If he made Lovelace less attractive to his readers (and many of the additions designed to blacken Lovelace's character are footnotes or other items that the reader of *Clarissa*, not Clarissa herself, would read), then they would be less inclined to believe that he was attractive to Clarissa. Richardson found it easier to alter the fictional world Clarissa inhabited than to rewrite the heroine herself.

In fact, as he got further from his experience of writing the novel, he became more immoderate in his claims for his heroine's independent existence and for her integrity and power as a role model.

My story is designed to strengthen the tender Mind, and to enable the worthy Heart to bear up against the Calamaties of Life. . . .

[5]When his readers found Lovelace so attractive that they pleaded for a happy ending to the novel, in which Lovelace would reform and Clarissa would marry him, Richardson inserted footnotes designed to blacken Lovelace's character. For a list of changes, see Shirley Van Marter, "Richardson's Revisions of *Clarissa* in the Second Edition," *Studies in Bibliography* 26 (1973): 107–32. For a discussion of these changes in the context of Richardson's relationship with Lady Bradshaigh, see the second section of this chapter.

Read my Story through and you will see that in the Example
Clarissa sets, Meekness of Heart is intirely consistent with that
Dignity of Mind, which on all proper Occasions she exerts with so
much distinguishing Excellence, as carried her above the irascible
Passions. (Carroll, 116)

The compulsion that led Richardson to write the novel also
fueled his attempts to control its interpretation as well as his
readers' treatment of his heroine. He spent years reading *Clarissa*, explaining the novel to his friends, revising it, and defend-
ing it against the same passionate and intrusive interpretations
his masterpiece impels its readers to make. Yet, in all of these
activities he behaved as a privileged intimate of his characters,
not as the author of all their complexities. A cursory reading of
his personal correspondence reveals many variants of the open-
ing, "Lovelace, I remember, told me once" (Carroll, 273), a
phrase that affects insouciance but betrays, by its very casual-
ness, some of the strain of Richardson's finding his voice only in
the guise of his fictional characters. One could call these casual
references to the "real" lives of his characters evidence of Richardson's naiveté, but it is more important to note that, because
there are so many of them, Richardson doesn't even write his
own letters in his own voice. All of his works, including the
Familiar Letters and much of the *Apprentice's Vade Mecum*, are
written in the first person, but never is that first person Richardson himself. This split is what allows Richardson to divide himself into the characters who penned the letters in *Clarissa* and the
printer who believed in them. And it means among other things
that the naive reader we encounter in Richardson's personal
letters is working in the service of the authors of the novel's
letters and directing our response to those letters.

Critics who haven't seen that Richardson's naiveté is situa-
tional and therefore limited have often claimed that Richardson
was only a gullible reader of the surface of his own novels who
remained unaware of the subtleties and the contradictions of the
novel that far outran his intentions. I propose to show, however,

that Richardson made great use of those contradictions even as they threatened to overwhelm him. This seems like a paradoxical assertion, but it is, in fact, only a recognition that the form of *Clarissa* prompts us to mistake Richardson for an unselfconscious reader of his own texts. His use of letters and in particular of the female voice is a deliberate misdirection of our interpretive or critical faculties that frees him to engage in the dazzling display that is *Clarissa*. And his guise as a seemingly accidental novelist alters his relationship to his readers. I contend that the ostensible artlessness of their creation makes Richardson's characters more captivating, and that Richardson regains on behalf of those fictional letter writers what—as an unsophisticated, fussy and overly pious didact—he loses in his own authorial person. More generally, Richardson's promulgation of his role as first reader (rather than first author) of his texts reveals how he went about creating a writing self and how the structures by which he did so defined that self. Moreover, these structural issues are all quite explicitly concerns of Richardson's. His personal correspondence and the novels themselves almost obsessively treat the issues of writerly authority and readerly interpretation as well as the mysteries of Richardson's own slippery authorial stance.

In this chapter I examine the mutual creation of Richardson's particular narrative structure and his authorial personae in three interconnected realms. In the next section I show how in his personal letters Richardson reveals the representational strategy of his novels by using that same fictional strategy in another context. In the second section I examine his relationship with his most devoted and challenging reader, Lady Bradshaigh, to show how he attempted to educate or coerce his readers into what he regarded as a proper response to his novel. The last section examines Richardson's attempts to direct our interpretation of his novels by posing as his own reader within the fictional text to reveal the ways in which the structures that serve Richardson so well also shape him.

The "Samuel Richardson" Persona

In his novels, Richardson uses the epistolary form to skirt the problem of creating a personal authorial voice. All of the voices in *Clarissa* are, of course, personal ones—that is, all of the letters and the editorial comments are written in the first person—but Richardson himself lays claim to none of them. Almost everyone in the book is an author, but the book itself has no author. Instead, *Clarissa* purports to be a collection of real letters, edited by John Belford and published for the edification of young ladies and their parents everywhere. Thus Richardson has created two fictional realities—the letters and the editorial comments—which buttress each other. The editor's access to the original letters gives power to his version of "The History of a Young Lady." The young lady's narrative gains authority through the interpretation provided by a respectable (and male) editor.[6] Richardson, shuttling between the two, taps the power of this paradoxical relationship he has set up between fiction and reality. I will return to this paradox as it is expressed in *Clarissa*. First I want to show how Richardson exploits it in his personal letters.

Richardson wrote perhaps as many letters to real recipients as he did to fictional ones. Toward the end of his life he claimed that writing had become irksome to him and that he had run out of imagination. In a letter to Sarah Chapone of 28 May 1754, he wrote, "The Indifference to the Pen, which I had at first struggled to obtain, has grown upon me to an Averseness to it; so that now Writing, even to my chosen Friends, is generally an irksome Task to me" (Carroll, 102).

[6]The term "editor," along with other seemingly simple terms like "writer" and "reader," acquires a certain ambiguity in the context of Richardson's novel. The only editor whose presence is wholly acknowledged in the text is John Belford. Richardson, however, appended the preface and the postscript and several footnotes whose perspective is clearly that of an editor outside of the fictional realm Belford inhabits. The most notable of these are the footnotes designed to blacken Lovelace's character, but there are countless other instances (and not all are confined to footnotes) where a meta-editor breaks into the text to direct our interpretation of characters and events.

His reference to his struggle to *obtain* an indifference to the pen betrays a certain ambivalence about the massive productions of that pen, but for most of his life, writing came far more easily to Richardson than speaking, and his letters to all the young women he set out to educate, to his friends, and to those of his readers who became friends all demonstrate his faith in the power and the enduring independence of this written word. As he writes to Sophia Westcomb in 1746, "Who then shall decline the converse of the pen? The pen that makes distance, presence; and brings back to sweet remembrance all the delights of presence; which makes even presence but body, while absence becomes the soul" (Carroll, 65).

For Richardson, the written word bridges the gap between fiction and reality and between absence and presence. His personal letters make clear that, while he was fully aware that he had created the fictional characters who populate his novels, he nevertheless believed in them. He reveals for his correspondents (and, quite consciously, for posterity[7]) the selves who wrote his novels, the selves who inhabited them, and the selves who read them. Ever the didact, he is teaching his correspondents the proper way to read his work.

He does so by readily discussing his characters, their motivations, and their fates. Both before and after publication he solicits advice about how those characters should behave. From women he asks for a truer view of the female heart. From those better educated or of a higher class he asks advice about the at-home behavior of the nobility. From all and sundry he wants confirmation that his tragic tale is morally instructive. Note, however, that he always rejects the advice he so plaintively requests, and that he never appeals to fellow novelists for any advice at all.

If we keep in mind the authorial strategies and structures of Richardson's fiction as we read his personal letters, we can see

---

[7]He even edited his correspondence with Lady Bradshaigh in anticipation of publishing it. See his letters to Lady Bradshaigh of 19 November 1757 and 2 January 1758 in Carroll, ed., *Selected Letters*, pp. 335–38.

that by appealing to his fictional characters to support his views on everything from the virtues of rising early to the proper limits on the ways his readers might interpret his novels, Richardson has found a way to pose as the editor of his personal letters. In this manner he is able to perpetuate the split that allows him to be passionately involved in his writing and yet to maintain some distance from it.

Furthermore, with this remarkable move, Richardson inserts his personal correspondence into the hierarchy of realistic fictions that make up his novels. His own letters, and the characters in them, are interleaved with the letters and characters in his novels and thus become part of the novelistic structure in which one fiction lends reality to another, embedded fiction. It becomes more and more difficult to tell, however, which fiction is the embedded one and therefore the "more" fictional. By treating Lovelace and Clarissa as real people in his personal letters, Richardson is actually inserting himself into their fictional world. That is, he can speak knowledgeably about these fictional characters, but he loses his substance as an author or a being who could exist (and write) outside the boundaries of his text.

His letters to Aaron Hill and other friends thus become no more and no less real than Anna Howe's letters to Clarissa. He writes to his friends and his real-world readers from within the fictional universe he has created and then decreed to be real. In a long letter to Lady Bradshaigh, for example, he moves easily from an authorlike discussion of strategy ("But let us suppose the Story to end, as you, Madam, would have it; what of extraordinary would there be in it?") to a thorough identification with his fictional world and his characters (" 'What a fine time of it,' as Lovelace says on this very Subject, 'would the Women have, if they were all to be put to the Test, as he puts Clarissa!' ") (Carroll, 103, 117). His "own" voice in his personal correspondence relies as much on the authority of his fictions as do his fictional voices on the historical and documentary trappings (letters, editors, footnotes, etc.) of the real world. Thus his personal letters have the same relationship to the text of *Clarissa* as Clarissa's story has to its editorial overlay. Furthermore, because Clarissa's and Lovelace's voices are his own creations, Richardson's ostensible appeal to "outside help" when he quotes from their letters blurs the boundary between inside and outside or self and other as effectively as that between real and fictional.

The obvious question is, What could Richardson say in the guise of his fictional characters that he could not say without them? A letter that Richardson wrote to his wife Elizabeth provides us with a partial answer. When he presented her with a bound copy of his massive novel *Clarissa*, he included a letter written on behalf of his heroine but signed with his own name. It is dated 1 December 1748.

> Dear Bett,
> Do you know, that the beatified CLARISSA was often very uneasy at the Time her Story cost the Man whom you favour with your Love; and that chiefly on your Account?
> She was.
> And Altho' she made not a posthumous Apology to you on that Account, as she did, on other Occasions, to several of those who far less deserved to be apologized to; I know so well her Mind, that she would have greatly approved of this Acknowledgement, and of the Compliment I now make you, in Her Name, of the Volumes which contain her History.
> May you, my dear Bett, May I, and all Ours, benefit by the Warnings, and by the Examples given in them!— And may our last Scenes be closed as happily as Her last Scene is represented to have done! Are the Prayers of
> Yours most affectionate
> Whilst
> S. Richardson (Carroll, 102)

This letter is a complicated and ambiguous document, which immediately throws into question the usual assumption that, as Terry Eagleton writes, "[Richardson's] pen exceeds his intentions, conjuring a . . . sub-text from beneath the carefully policed script of his novel."[8] He may be policing his novel, but the

---

[8]Terry Eagleton, *The Rape of Clarissa: Writing, Sexuality, and Class Struggle in Samuel Richardson* (Minneapolis: University of Minnesota Press, 1982), pp. 77–78.

Richardson of this and so many other private letters also displays a subtle and playful understanding of the subtext and of the powerful impact that the fictional Clarissa has had on his identity. More important for our reading of the novel, the author "Whilst S. Richardson" is very clearly toying with the boundaries between author and character, male and female, and artist and audience by which his critics have generally presumed him to be circumscribed.

In the letter to Bett, for example, the real-world Richardson who might be supposed to be writing this letter to his wife has become the insubstantial, almost fictional character, ceding before the epistolary power of the "beatified CLARISSA." Richardson portrays himself as, at best, a lowly admirer privileged to be Clarissa's scribe, a mere mediator for his heroine's direct address to his wife, and her apology for "the Time her Story cost the Man whom you favour with your Love."

In fact, Richardson is using Clarissa as the mediator of his love for his wife. He presents his compliments to his wife in Clarissa's name, and he claims the right to do so because he "know[s] so well her Mind, that she would have greatly approved of this Acknowledgement." Thus, for the authority to write his wife an apologetic love letter, Richardson appeals to a fictional character he has created and then "beatified."

Not until the letter's closing salutation does Richardson make reference to his role as the author of Clarissa's being, and then only in the nicely ambiguous use of "Whilst." Certainly that closing is a reference to his being Samuel Richardson only "whilst" he is a mere mortal awaiting his last scene, after which he will return to dust. But in literary terms he is also Samuel Richardson only when he is not Clarissa, and he is not Samuel Richardson when he is writing as Clarissa. In his progress back and forth between the two, he ends up, as in this deceptively simple letter, masquerading as himself. The masquerade gives him a voice. "Whilst S. Richardson," he is a good Christian and a loving husband, but he is not an author—that he only is, in a sense, "whilst" other people. He achieves artistic and literary power by publicly abdicating his right to tell his own story and by denying his ability to write a letter in his own person. Significantly, Richardson uses the letter form, for it is the structural absence (of the correspondent) that motivates the writing of a letter. This structural absence enables Richardson to disguise his authorship of his texts and to distance and defuse the problems any writer faces by thematizing them as battles over pen, paper, and interpretation in his novels. I will further explore this paradoxical writing from the abyss and its relationship to the crucial absence of authority that motivates *Clarissa* in the third section of this chapter. At this point I want to concentrate on the ways in which Richardson's personal letters mirror and explicate the fictional letters that make up his novels.

Since the letter is an intimate form that demands a high degree of involvement from its readers yet is always public by virtue of its staged quality and its potential as a historical document, it provides an ideal environment for Richardson's narrative maneuvers.[9] It allows him to make a great claim on our sympathies while exploiting the artifice of this seemingly most artless form of writing. The letters that make up *Clarissa* are ostensibly private and often confessional in tone. Yet, the sheer length of the novel reinforces its theatrical quality. That length is in part the effect of his famous "writing to the moment," Richardson claims. "Nineteen or Twenty Vols. Closely printed! A Man of Business too!—Monstrous! . . . All I have to say for myself is . . . that the new Manner of Writing—to the Moment—betray'd me into it; flattering myself, that hardly any-one, who would attempt the

[9]For more on the theory of the letter and the particular tension between the epistle and novel forms, see Janet Altman, *Epistolarity: Approaches to a Form* (Columbus: Ohio State University Press, 1982); Margaret Anne Doody, *A Natural Passion: A Study of the Novels of Samuel Richardson* (Oxford: Clarendon Press, 1974); Bruce Redford, *The Converse of the Pen: Acts of Intimacy in the Eighteenth-Century Familiar Letter* (Chicago: University of Chicago Press, 1986); and William B. Warner, *Reading "Clarissa": The Struggles of Interpretation* (New Haven: Yale University Press, 1979). I disagree with the details of several of these readings. In particular, Warner's argument makes Clarissa the active author in the text and attributes the text's inconsistencies to her attempts to mislead both Lovelace and her external readers. He thus occludes Richardson's role as author of the text.

same Manner, would be able to avoid the same Excess" (Carroll, 329).

But that very technique of writing to the moment is the epitome of disingenuous artfulness: the author attempts to disarm his readers' critical faculties by structuring Pamela's prose so that it will seem spontaneous and unedited. And as Henry Fielding's parody *Shamela* shows, it takes very little exaggeration to turn Pamela's supposedly innocent babble into a calculated theatrics of virginity. Yet Richardson's pen also truly ran away with him. In *Clarissa*, Lovelace and Clarissa and even Clarissa's uncles and her Cousin Morden seize it to engage in highly dramatic displays of themselves and their versions of events. Richardson was left both proud of and abashed by his prolixity. In the novels he is prolix in the guise of Lovelace or Pamela or Harriet Byron; in his personal correspondence some of those scribbling personae are named Samuel Richardson.

Richardson himself was well aware that he was somehow more than himself in writing. His own letters portray him as awkward and tongue-tied in personal encounters. Yet he managed to turn even that failure of his voice into an occasion for seduction in writing. A letter to Lady Bradshaigh, perhaps next to Richardson the most involved and argumentative reader of *Clarissa*, opens rather petulantly but soon reaches a peak of coyly innocent flirtation:

> Mr. . . . is certainly a worthy Man. He has not written to me since he left London. I suppose I answered not, on a personal Acquaintance, the *too* high Ideas he had of me from what I had published. I am always jealous of suffering in the Opinion of my Readers, when we come into personal Conversation . . . Let me own to you, that I never paid my personal Duty to your Ladiship, but I came away half dissatisfied with myself, from the Diffidence I have mentioned; and glad at my Heart was I, when the next Visit from your Ladiship, or Command to attend you, gave me Hope, that your Goodness had not permitted me to sink in your Favour. In writing, I own, I was always an impudent Man. But need I tell your Ladiship that? (13 August 1755 [Carroll, 319])

Even in his letters to his friends, Richardson rarely writes "as himself." He defers instead to the voices of his fictional characters, quoting "their" views to reinforce his stated opinions, as if he had not also penned the text from which he now cites as from some unimpeachable source: "See how Colonel Morden judges on this very Subject" or "as Lovelace says on this very Subject" (Carroll, 114). The subject, of course, is women and matrimony, and Richardson's quoting from these "authorities" is one small example of the almost unfathomable ironies of the author's relation to *Clarissa* and Clarissa. I will venture deeper into ironies later. For the moment it is enough to note that the same man who created Lovelace and later felt the need to blacken his character nevertheless refers to the authority of this sadistic rake when discussing the proper behavior of an honorable man toward the women he has seduced.

More often Richardson quotes Clarissa herself (of course "herself" is an ambiguous term in this context). In October 1748 he wrote: "Hear what my Girl says on that Subject, writing to her dear Friend Miss Howe, to comfort her on her apparent Decline" (Carroll, 91). Here the subject is the worthlessness of earthly life, and at the moment that Richardson quotes from "his Girl," he has ceded his earthly life to her. In the process he becomes his own ideally receptive and passionate reader, one who can pray in another context that his and Bett's "last Scenes be closed as happily as [Clarissa's] last Scene is represented to have done!" As Samuel Richardson he is a reader, an admirer, and sometimes an editor, but not a writer. The writer is named Clarissa or Pamela or Lovelace.

Richardson expected his readers to accept his shadowy presence as an editor within his texts without trying to pin down his authorial role. In his letters to his friends, Richardson jealously guards his status as a privileged reader and an authoritative interpreter of his novels ("I know so well Her Mind"), but he resists attempts to specify any closer relationship between himself and his heroines such as locating the source of female narrators in his own biography or calling himself to account for their wayward behavior.

In a long autobiographical letter to Johannes Stinstra, his Dutch translator, Richardson denies that he acquired any female sympathies from his youthful experience as amanuensis to young women carrying on love intrigues. He asserts, rather, that this experience prompted only a properly male intellectual and abstract investigation of the female heart:

> You think, Sir, you can account from my early secretaryship to young women in my father's neighborhood, for the characters I have drawn of the heroines of my three works. But this opportunity did little more for me, at so tender an age, than point, as I may say, or lead my inquiries, as I grew up, into the knowledge of the female heart. (Carroll, 297)

Richardson's distance from his characters, most notably his female letter writers, fluctuates. When he responds to his correspondents' criticism or admiration of his heroines, he adopts in turn the positions of: another reader, viewing his texts from a position analogous to if slightly more elevated than his correspondent's; the detached craftsman, an inquirer "into the knowledge of the female heart"; and a passionate advocate for his own work and the characters he believes in. What these stances have in common is that each of them allows Richardson to instruct us on the proper way to read his work. From his more or less concealed position as exemplary reader, distanced editor, or involved author, Richardson attempts to direct our interpretive activity from within the text of his novels.

Once again his personal correspondence reveals most clearly the structures by which he invents his ideal reader. His letters abound with examples of how his credulous fleshing out of his imaginary creatures (no less genuine for being dimly acknowledged as naive) coexists with a canny manipulation of his readers into an imitation of his own kind of reading, in particular of his own uncritical reception of his heroine. As he writes to his erstwhile admiring reader Aaron Hill: "As to Clarissa's being in downright love, I must acknowledge, that I rather would have it imputed to her, ([Lovelace's] too well-known Character consider'd) by her penetrating Friend, (and then a Reader will be ready enough to believe it, the more ready, for her not owning it, or being blind to it herself) than to think *her self* that she is" (Carroll, 72).

The intent of this sentence is hard to sort out. Its convoluted, back-and-forth structure mirrors the authorial task Richardson has set for himself: he has to remain on the move, situating authority in first one narrator and then another, if his novels are to avoid collapsing in upon their central absence, that place where the author should be. This is also, of course, the movement of narrative transvestism, in which an authoritative authorial voice is created through an elaborate cycle of abdications.

Richardson simultaneously acknowledges the demands that the structure of his novel makes of its readers. We have to hold in suspension all of the related perspectives that make this quotation so grammatically awkward. And the net effect is to make us all "if not Authors, Carpers." A "Carper" is, of course, an interpreter of the novel. But Richardson, having given us this responsibility, is anxious to make us exercise it in the proper way and toward the proper ends. Hence the insistence on the simple moral that is not borne out by his complex story, and hence the many structural devices which aim to push us in the right interpretive direction. I will return to these devices, and to their thematization in the general misinterpretation of Clarissa's letters by her readers within the novel, in the third section of this chapter.

Richardson's correspondence shows the strain of his fictional technique in other ways. We can see his moral and emotional involvement at war with the more distant perspective of the craftsman. When Aaron Hill wrote to him accusing Clarissa of "voluntarily running away from her Father's house" (Carroll, 82), Richardson was torn between blaming Hill for being an inattentive reader and blaming himself for being an inadequate craftsman. Richardson's blind defense of Clarissa—a captivating characteristic of his reading self and a dangerous trait of his editing self—is manifested here in the tortured syntax of his reply to Hill.

But I am very greatly mortified, that I have so much laboured, as to make it manifest, that Clarissa, tho' provoked as she was by a disgraceful Confinement; . . . that, althou' she would stay, she would die rather than be compelled to be the Man's Wife she hated; That this should be called, by such a clear Discerner; *a rash Elopement with a Man;* . . . I am very unfortunate, good Sir, let me say, to be so ill-understood: To have given reason, I should say, to be so little understood. (Carroll, 82)

The letter ends with a petulant threat never to publish *Clarissa* at all. "I have no Intention to trouble the World for its Opinion; and am only sorry for the Trouble and Perplexity I have given by it to a Gentleman to whom I wish to be able to give Pleasure, and nothing else" (Carroll, 83–84).

Of course Richardson did publish *Clarissa*, but he insulated Clarissa's text beneath many layers of reading and interpretation. The overlapping conjunctions and contradictions of these internal interpretations produce a text that demonstrates that reading is a complicated activity, even while its author insists (in the preface, for example) that literature is didactic and reading quite simply imitative. For this reason he is careful to note that Lovelace and Belford are not "infidels or scoffers," and that the story of Clarissa will not interfere with its didactic purpose:

But it is not amiss to premise, for the sake of such as may ap-prehend hurt to the morals of youth from the more freely-written letters, that the gentlemen, though professed libertines as to the fair sex, and making it one of their wicked maxims to keep no faith with any of the individuals of it who throw themselves into their power, are not, however, either infidels or scoffers; nor yet such as think themselves freed from the observance of other moral obliga-tions.

In all works of this, and of the dramatic kinds, *story* or *amusement* should be considered as little more than the vehicle to the more necessary *instruction*.[10]

Still, Richardson could also demonstrate a surprisingly playful awareness of his game of authorial hide-and-seek. He used his

[10]Richardson, *Clarissa*, pp. 35, 36.

talent for being absorbed in his characters to disclaim responsibility for their actions and, of course, for his own as their
author. Responding to Lady Bradshaigh's criticism of his satiric
description of an old woman, he writes:

> Was It I that dressed Aunt Nell? Fie upon me! I ought *never to be
> forgiven* . . . But how can it be said I and not Charlotte dressed
> Aunt Nell?—Here I sit down to form characters. One I intend to be
> all goodness; All goodness he is. . . . I am all the while absorbed in
> the character. It is not fair to say—I, identically am any-where,
> while I keep within the character. And if I have done so, why say
> you, madam, that I dressed Aunt Nell? But after all, give me leave
> to say, that a *Lady* who ridicules Old Maids is far less excusable
> than a man. (Carroll, 286)

The twists and turns of this teasing caveat, which finally becomes an attack (and it is hard to say whether the *"Lady"* being
chastised is the fictional character in *Sir Charles Grandison*, Lady
Bradshaigh, or her pseudonymous self, Belfour[11]), are remarkably similar to the coy admissions and evasive disclaimers of
Richardson's autobiographical letter to Stinstra. In both cases
Richardson demonstrates an extraordinary concern with the reception of his fictional personae—and his life—by his readers.

He is torn, as always, between his need to entice his readers
into intense involvement with his characters, and his desire to
foreordain the outcome of such converse between reader and
character. And so he wants to be "everywhere" and "nowhere"
in his texts at the same time; he is everywhere masked and
nowhere—that is to say only in the gaps between masks—
unmasked.

Note, however, that Richardson gives up none of his per-
quisites as an author. Despite his nervous and clever disclaimer,
Richardson is, of course, everywhere in his texts, even while he
"keep[s] within the character." His abdication of authorial con-

---

[11]"Belfour" is the name Lady Bradshaigh used when she initiated the correspondence with Richardson. In the next section I discuss the use of the pseudonym and
its similarity to the name "Belford."

trol is a mask that enables his powerful presence as an editor and exemplary reader.

In another letter to Lady Bradshaigh, who was a tireless advocate for giving *Clarissa* a conventionally happy ending, he writes, "If Clarissa think not an early Death an Evil, but on the contrary, after an exemplary Preparation, looks upon it as her consummating Perfection, who shall grudge it her?—Who shall punish her with Life?" (Carroll, 95–96). Although Richardson has, in some sense, created Clarissa only to silence her or to co-opt her voice, his genuine susceptibility to his creation also infuses her with an independent life. And by submerging himself in "her" life, Richardson vicariously lives out his own life as an author. He writes her in order to read her, and his reading of her is both an act of homage and one of tyrannical interpretation.

In the face of his recalcitrant or overeager readers, Richardson sometimes found it hard to maintain this double stance. He pretended to be the editor of Clarissa's letters so that he could disguise his creative activity as mere editing—that is, as reading. Yet he felt compelled to defend his heroine against her critics, and those attempts often left him uncomfortably constrained by one or the other extreme of the paradoxical structure by which he maintained both his art and his artlessness or, in the terms of his literary activity, his authorial and readerly selves.

That final phrase, "Who shall punish her with Life?," is of the same order as his wish that he and Bett might learn from Clarissa's example how to welcome their deaths. Here Richardson is being his own ideal reader, and Clarissa's book is a kind of practical bible for him—a handbook on how best to conduct oneself while beset by the evils and the constraints of the earthly life. Clearly—and this is where Richardson the artist exploits the felicitous discoveries of his reading self—that same phrase ("Who shall . . . ") is also a warning to Lady Bradshaigh and to other similarly interested readers about the proper limits of their interpretive activity. As such it is an assertion of authorial power embedded in an admission of powerlessness, a promulgation of rules for readers embedded in a humble submission to those same rules. Because he "know[s] so well her Mind," Clarissa gives him the authority to resist Lady Bradshaigh's interpretations.

Educating Lady Bradshaigh

Lady Dorothy Bradshaigh introduced herself to Richardson by letter under the pseudonym of "Belfour."[12] She had read the first four volumes of *Clarissa* and was so upset at rumors that the novel would end with the heroine's death that she wrote Richardson a letter of protest. She left the letter for him at a shop and requested that he reply by an advertisement in a newspaper. Richardson did reply and found a reader who was as deeply concerned with Clarissa's fate as he was himself. Lady Bradshaigh was his very own Lovelace—a seducer, tyrant, and worthy opponent who was yet a devotee. Her very choice of pseudonym (so like that of Clarissa's editor, the converted rake Belford) presages her desire to be converted to Richardson's reading of Clarissa's life as a Christian triumph. Yet her battles with him over the fate of his heroine allowed Richardson to enact the continuing engulfment of his life by his fiction and to find— as he habitually did—his direction and his voice against opposition and otherness.

The shared passion of these letter writers was the fate of an epistolary relationship between fictional characters whose lives

---

[12]The spelling of this pseudonym varies according to the account of the relationship. John Traugott refers to "Belcour." Eaves and Kimpel uses "Belfour," which I have adopted in part because of its clear similarity to "Belford." Linda Kauffman uses "Balfour." Whether or not it is also based on some confusion about eighteenth-century orthography, it seems clear that "Belcour" has the coy tone that Traugott is seeking. Few of Richardson's critics have failed to take note of his epistolary relationship with Lady Bradshaigh. I refer primarily to the versions offered by Eaves and Kimpel and by Traugott. Terry Castle, *Clarissa's Ciphers*; Eagleton, *Rape of Clarissa*; T. C. Duncan Eaves and Ben D. Kimpel, *Samuel Richardson: A Biography* (Oxford: Clarendon Press, 1971); and Linda S. Kauffman, *Discourses of Desire: Gender, Genre, and Epistolary Fictions* (Ithaca: Cornell University Press, 1986). See also other books and articles on Richardson in the bibliography.

were more real to "Belfour" and the "publisher" of Clarissa's letters than their own lives could have been. Their letters, and Richardson's replies to Lady Bradshaigh's marginal notations in her copy of *Clarissa*, are an intricate and resonant working out of the relationships between author, text, and reader that *Clarissa* engenders. Like the novel itself, their correspondence takes dazzling risks as they both analyze and mirror the letters between Lovelace and Clarissa. At times they seemed to be unable to tell their own epistolary world from that of the novel.[13] The critic runs a similar risk in assuming a simple equation between the two rather than exploring a more complex relationship between reader, author, and text.

John Traugott's account of Richardson's relationship to Lady Bradshaigh is too simplistic, for example.[14] Although he uses the relationship to illustrate some observations that are not so different from my own, he ignores the issues raised by a consideration of gender and of the transgression of gender boundaries in narrative. Traugott recognizes that Richardson "forced the reader to participate with him in the artifice of his own imaginings" (164) and that Richardson was balancing two contradictory impulses (Traugott calls them his comic sense and his moral sincerity). But these observations are ultimately put in the service of an argument that Richardson was only an "incessant sexual moral[izer]—always banal and often nasty" (157).

A nice little flirtation of the porcine printer and the sentimental lady. What a pair!—he the self-appointed dominie to the king-

---

[13]As part of her argument about the activity of the reader of *Clarissa* in constructing the novel, Castle makes this point on p. 49n of *Clarissa's Ciphers:* "Lady Bradshaigh described one proposed meeting between them as a way of turning 'a certain imaginary scene into reality,' yet the difficulties they had achieving this end suggest their unwillingness to let go of their 'textual' preconceptions of each other." While I agree with many of the particulars of Castle's argument, I don't agree that Richardson ultimately abdicates his authorial power. That abdication is rather an intermediate step in the process of directing his readers' activity.

[14]John Traugott, "*Clarissa*'s Richardson: An Essay to Find the Reader," in *English Literature in the Age of Disguise,* ed. Maximilian E. Novak (Berkeley: University of California Press, 1977), pp. 157–208. Page references are in parentheses in the text.

dom's nice ladies, feeding their little vanities with compliments to their delicacies and with avuncular advice (though always with that supercilious eye) about their maidenly or conjugal duties; she his mysterious admirer from afar, weeping a "pint of tears," as she put it, for Clarissa's hard fate and petitioning by post that her famous author-correspondent should soften his heart and undo the mischief that Lovelace had already done on Clarissa's body. . . . We need not think we catch Richardson out in this little comedy. He knows what he is doing. It is the same teasing sensibility that is working out the structure of *Clarissa*. (159–60)[15]

Although Traugott asserts at the end of this account that "we need not think we catch Richardson out in this little comedy," that is clearly what this rather sensational account aims to do. His reading of *Clarissa* is limited by this effort to expose the dirty secrets beneath the piousness of both the book's heroine and its author.

With Traugott, I think that Richardson, even in his most self-indulgent fantasies, could not have invented a more susceptible reader than Lady Bradshaigh or one who so particularly shared his penchant for flirtatious epistolary sparring. The matter does not end there, however. As their letters show, they were both

---

[15]Traugott's account begins: "The mere physiognomy of Richardson imposes a ridiculous puppet between us and the great author of *Clarissa*. We must see him as he saw himself in that little travesty of a Restoration comedy he wrote in his correspondence with Lady Bradshaigh—or with Belcour, as she coyly called herself. There he is walking in St. James's Park, up and down the alleys, every day, three or four hours at a time, this plump little man, five-foot-five, fair wig riding atop a long black cloak (for his health is none of the best), looking straight on (but noticing all sides), never turning his short fat neck, despite eyes misted over by a rheum from his head, missing none of the ladies; feet that trot beneath the large hoops passing in the alley. That supercilious eye of his, he says, as the thought of hoops and little feet revives him. He is having a sort of tryst, even assignation, with the mysterious Belcour; though thus far they have exchanged only teasingly sentimental letters, she has given him to understand that she too will be walking in the park unperceived. Which hoop is she?, which little feet? Will she reveal herself? She will not say" (ibid., 159).

For a more sober account of Richardson's relationship with Lady Bradshaigh, see Eaves and Kimpel, *Samuel Richardson*, pp. 221–34. Traugott is not alone, however, in identifying what he sees as Richardson's fumblings with Lady Bradshaigh with his fumblings as a novelist. See, for example, Carroll's introduction to the letters and Eagleton's analysis in *Rape of Clarissa* (esp. pp. 26–28), which identifies class difference as the source of those "fumblings."

aware of the game they were playing—not only of its coy sexual content, but also of its deliberate blurring of the boundaries between fiction and reality. Moreover, Lady Bradshaigh's tenacity in her arguments about Clarissa's fate eventually amounted to a challenge to Richardson's authorial position, and in his rebukes to her, he asserts both his authority over *Clarissa* and his conception of the boundaries to readerly participation more clearly than in any other circumstance. Thus the two letter writers both play out and deliberately play with the thematic and structural issues of writing and interpretation that Richardson poses in *Clarissa*. Richardson makes explicit the role he conceived for *Clarissa*'s readers, and he fights off one kind of challenge to the limits of that role.[16]

Yet he also encourages that challenge. Richardson shows more clearly in his correspondence with Lady Bradshaigh than anywhere else how he masks himself to facilitate unmasking himself. He draws her attention to his various masks and by so doing, hints at the unknown self behind them. For example, while commiserating with Lady Bradshaigh's desire to see Clarissa happy on earth, Richardson tosses off a comment that functions as a remarkable gloss on his attempts to construct an ideal reader of *Clarissa*. Within the novel that ideal reader is the editor (both Belford and the shadowy Richardson). In his letters to Lady Bradshaigh, Richardson is trying to train her for that position by teaching her that she is only *Clarissa*'s reader and not the author of the heroine's fate. In both epistolary universes Richardson sheds his authorial guise and re-creates himself as an internal (and so less authoritarian, more seductive) guide to the wayward reader. In this sense Traugott's point (that Richardson

[16]The issues raised by gender in reading and writing also weave in and out of this epistolary mutual seduction. From the accounts that I have read, Richardson does not seem to have been in doubt for long about the sex of his mysterious admirer, but it is interesting to speculate about Lady Bradshaigh's intentions in choosing a distinctly masculine pseudonym and about any resulting lingering ambiguity in their relationship. In any event, Lady Bradshaigh's higher social status would have complicated the expected power relationship between male author and sentimental female reader.

teases Lady Bradshaigh just as Clarissa and Lovelace tease each other and *Clarissa* teases its readers) is true.

In writing of himself as a reader of his own novel—in particular of Clarissa's suffering—Richardson admits: "Nor can I go thro' some of the Scenes myself without being sensibly touched (Did I not say, that I was another Pygmalion?)" (Carroll, 90). That parenthetical coy confession, "(Did I not say, that I was another Pygmalion?),'' is an extraordinarily complicated one. Granted, if one sets out to view Richardson as an unconscious "natural" writer, then one might well also say that his involvement with his characters is further proof of his lack of self-awareness. For Richardson himself to point to that involvement with a knowing air, however, is another matter entirely. For Pygmalion is not unselfaware as an artist; rather he is unselfaware as a lover. Moreover, if Richardson has enough self-knowledge to claim he is "another Pygmalion," then he cannot really be one. He chooses, rather, to be unselfaware when unselfconsciousness will aid the novelist. In the world of the novel, the editor is self-aware and the letter writer is not; men are self-aware, women are not. But in the world of *Clarissa*, all self-awareness is relative; one cannot read the book without becoming to some degree a Pygmalion. Moreover, by so consistently transgressing the boundaries between editor and letter writer, and between male interpretations of female texts, Richardson further complicates the positions of both author and reader. Lady Bradshaigh, as the particular reader to whom his comment about Pygmalion is directed, is left balancing between being an encroaching reader and a silly sentimental woman. As one response to her as the former, we have Richardson's "testy" replies to her marginal notations in her own copy of *Clarissa*, rather like Lovelace's angry pointing fingers in the margins of Anna Howe's letter exposing Lovelace's true character (L. 229.1).[17] For the latter, we

---

[17]Richardson, *Clarissa*, pp. 743–52. The word "testy" is from the description of Lady Bradshaigh's copy of *Clarissa*, which was offered for sale in Bernard Quaritch's Catalogue #1083, Fall 1987, pp. 36–38. "L 229.1" indicates a letter enclosed within letter 229.

have Traugott's condemnation of her as a "goose" ("*Clarissa*'s
Richardson," 171).

In his version of the myth of Pygmalion, Ovid comments
archly on the artist's self-abandonment by moving from Pygmalion's perspective, "The image seemed / That of a virgin,
truly, almost living," to that of an uninvolved spectator, "The
best art, they say, / Is that which conceals art, and so Pygmalion /
Marvels, and loves the body he has fashioned."[18] Richardson's
parentheses accomplish the same change of voice and the same
ironic perspective. From the relatively uncomplicated confession that he is "sensibly touched" by his own creation, he moves
to a parenthetical realm that contains two different perspectives
on himself and his work. The phrase "Did I not say" affects an
offhandedness that attempts to conceal the power of his confession, "I was another Pygmalion." In this brief parenthetical
phrase Richardson strains to be both Pygmalion and Ovid, both
the dupe of his own art and the ironic commentator on his own
susceptibility. But the two perspectives cannot be comfortably
expressed by the same voice. In *Clarissa* he parcels out the conflict among different characters and different editorial levels in
the text. The tension works as a motivating force on both the
thematic and the structural levels.

When he is writing to Lady Bradshaigh, Richardson resolves
this same tension by scripting her role in the dialogue and defining his own role against hers. Lady Bradshaigh is a willing, if not
always predictable, participant in this mutually creative inter-
penetration of their personal correspondence with the fictional
correspondence in *Clarissa*. In fact, she laid the groundwork for it
with her initial letter about Clarissa's impending death. She
recognized that the book's author could change Clarissa's fate,
yet she wanted that fate altered because Clarissa was real to her.
For her, as for Richardson, *Clarissa* was both a work of art and
an artifact of nature. Richardson is both captivated by her re-

[18]Ovid, *Metamorphoses*, trans. Rolfe Humphries (Bloomington: Indiana University
Press, 1955), pp. 241–43 (Book 10, lines 243–96).

ceptivity and anxious to set limits to her participation in his Pygmalion-like activity. By moralizing about her attachment to Clarissa, he clearly ranks her with the statue rather than with the sculptor. By setting the boundaries to her readerly activity, he reminds her that she is, at least when she writes to him as Belfour, as much his creation as her own. One of the ways he does this is by changing the terms of the dialogue. In the same letter in which he admits to being another Pygmalion, he insists that *Clarissa* is not a work of art but a didactic tool: "Such are the Lessons I endeavour to inculcate by an Example in natural Life. And the more irksome these Lessons are to the Young, the Gay, and the Healthy, the more necessary are they to be inculcated" (Carroll, 91).

Richardson resolves his own conflict by chastising Lady Bradshaigh for her susceptibility and for her inattention to the Christian moral of his novel. "And what Madam, is the temporary Happiness we are so fond of? What the long Life we are so apt to covet?" (Carroll, 91). Richardson is writing to Lady Bradshaigh, but he is also writing *through* her to himself. She, like Clarissa, is his other and his own creation. He moves between the two perspectives in the same way that he moves between the off-handedness of "Did I not say" and the self-exposure of "I was another Pygmalion."

That same combination encompasses the movement of their coy epistolary dance in which self-revelation is accomplished through disguise, and seduction through withdrawal. Richardson's confession is tossed off as if he were saying to his Belfour, Did you not notice this obvious thing? He draws closer to her when he admits that he shares her susceptibility, and then he reasserts his difference from her by pointing out that his susceptibility is a measure of his power as a writer, while hers makes her a reader who has missed the moral of the story. Thus he sets the boundaries of interpretation. If she stays within the form of his discourse, Lady Bradshaigh can only assent to Richardson's insight. She cannot dispute or reinterpret it, nor can she continue to insist that her own special love for Clarissa gives her any privileged rights over the character's fate.

Richardson's declaration that he is another Pygmalion, however, is also more true than he can acknowledge. He is most fully
a blind lover of his creation when he obsessively defends Clarissa (and *Clarissa*) against even the smallest criticism. He is particularly scornful of those women (like Lady Bradshaigh) who
"give too much Countenance to Men of the vile Cast . . . the
greater Vulgar, as well as all the less, [who] had rather it had had
what they call, an Happy Ending."[19]

This display of misogyny is uncomfortably like Lovelace's
willful misinterpretation of Clarissa.[20] And this likeness is not by
accident; misogyny is clearly the fuel for the initial impetus to
create a perfect woman—an other who is simultaneously a self.
If we return to the myth of Pygmalion, we find that Pygmalion's
love for the ivory statue he has created "with marvelous art" (l.
248) is also narcissistic and born of a disgust for real women. He
"had seen these women / Leading their shameful lives, shocked
at the vices / Nature has given the female disposition" (ll. 243–
45). This is not so different from the impulse to remake woman
in his own image that prompted Richardson to create heroines
that could serve as exemplars to the morally frail sex. In a letter
to Sarah Chapone in August of 1758, Richardson reiterates his
view that

> the delicate Sex . . . when called to act themselves and not to
> judge upon the Actions of others, if weighted in the Scale of strict
> Propriety, will be often found wanting. Why, let me tell you,
> Madam . . . there are in my poor Writings, in each of the three
> Pieces, an Hundred Instances that the Sex for whose Service they
> were chiefly written, pass over, as so many Incomprehensibles to
> them. (Carroll, 340)

He similarly takes Lady Bradshaigh to task in the pages of her
own annotated copy of *Clarissa*. As he replies to her comments

[19]Quoted in Eaves and Kimpel, *Samuel Richardson*, pp. 217–18.
[20]Castle makes this point in *Clarissa's Ciphers*: "There is a certain irony here:
Richardson patronizingly ascribes to his female readers precisely that sort of flighty
bad judgement and sexual *faiblesse* that his heroine's fictional persecutors belabor *her*
with—and his remarks carry an unpleasant burden of unacknowledged, almost
Lovelacean misogyny" (173). Richardson's personal correspondence provides countless other examples of his misogyny. See in particular his chiding letters to young
women friends.

one by one, he is making his ultimate intrusion into the space of the reader. He couches it, predictably, in terms of a defense of her incursion into his text. He accepts her judgment in matters of class taste (such as a change from "excuse" to "pardon"), but when she suggests that Lovelace's duplicity and bad manners are overdone, he replies, "Surely Madam, if you had consider'd all that is said in this passage only, you would not have made this Remark." He doesn't defend his book so much as he deflects the energy of her interpretation of it with comments such as *"Device!*—I don't love your Ladiship just here! Poor Clarissa!" and "O Ma-damn!"[21] In her willingness to be defined and her refusal to be silenced by him, Lady Bradshaigh proved an ideal match for Richardson. While he educated her about the proper way to read *Clarissa*, she played out with him his delight in readerly transgression and his fears about the ability of his creation to stand on its own.

Reading the Body of the Text:
Clarissa and Narrative Transvestism

While the degree of Lady Bradshaigh's involvement with *Clarissa* and with its heroine's fate may have been extraordinary, the fact of that involvement and the form it took were both dictated by the text. Richardson wants to entice every reader into an intimate relationship with his characters; this is why *Clarissa* is so much about reading and interpretation. We are all to become if not authors, carpers. And being carpers (but not authors) will make us proper readers of Clarissa's story. We have already seen how Richardson invited Lady Bradshaigh into his fictional world and then attempted to define the extent of her incursion. In the same way he carefully defines an enticing but limited space within *Clarissa* for every external reader to inhabit. He structures his epistolary text around a crucial absence of authority, creating

---

[21]Lady Bradshaigh's notes and Richardson's replies are quoted in the Bernard Quaritch catalogue.

a kind of interpretive vacuum for us to fill. Then, by taking the battle between men and women over that same authority as his theme, he ensures that our engagement with the novel implicates us in the characters' struggles over the relationships between speech, gender, and authority. Thus our critical faculties are both stimulated and compromised—every attempt to unravel the structure of the novel leads us back into the complex and ironic suggestiveness of Richardson's narrative transvestism.

In *Clarissa*, Richardson has created a world in which the terms of all discourse are unstable, and in which writing, reading, and the identification of a gendered self are, thus, political acts, fraught with the anxiety of self-assertion and the curse of self-limitation. Letter writing, for example, becomes an act of defiance against patriarchal authority (for Clarissa) or an act of tyranny or transvestism (for Lovelace). Reading such letters can never be a neutral act: the internal readers in the novel are all interested parties in the battle, which is ostensibly over property and marriage. In fact, the sexes are at war over who shall control the materials of the writer: pen and paper, text and interpretation, the expressive self and the body that confines it. But, as in any protracted war, it is soon difficult to make any clear distinction between the opponents. And when Richardson writing as Anna Howe fulminates against the male sex, or writing as Lovelace forges a letter from Clarissa, he is deliberately complicating on a structural level (that is, the level perceived by external readers) the distinction between male and female utterance that is so crucial to the plot and to his characters' interpretations of each others' letters.[22] Thus every external reader of *Clarissa* is also an interested party, and willy-nilly they stand in for that absent internal authority.

Clearly, if we are to examine the impact of Richardson's structural and thematic concern with narrative transvestism upon his novel, we need to distinguish between the activity of internal

[22]For a discussion of eighteenth-century England's concepts of gender, gendered speech, and the transgression of gender's boundaries, see Chapter 1.

fictional readers and external ones. The several layers of fictional editors make this distinction a tricky one at times, but we can specify the questions the novel compels each set of readers to ask. For *Clarissa's* internal readers, the urgent questions upon which so much of the text turns might be formulated as: What is permitted speech for a woman? and, If a woman crosses the boundaries of permitted speech, is she still a woman? For external readers these questions become: Where does interpretation stop and tyranny begin? and, What is the relationship between the body and effective speech? In this section I first examine the dynamic of narrative transvestism as it is reflected in the struggles within *Clarissa* to find a balance between self and other, male and female, and interpretation and writing. I then add the structural overlay of Richardson's narrative transvestism to those thematic struggles. Of course that structural overlay colors my discussion of the novel; it reveals how the plot doubles over on itself and how every conflict is essentially an exchange of power between gendered voices.

The characters' anxious search for interpretive authority is made explicit in the novel's very first letter, from Miss Anna Howe to Miss Clarissa Harlowe, voicing her desire for "the authority of your own information" and dread of "your directors and directresses; for your mamma, admirably well qualified as she is to lead, must submit to be led. Your sister and brother will certainly put you out of your course."[23] The rest of the novel might fairly be characterized as the working out of the implications of this passage.

Anna requests Clarissa's version of events, but in fact, in the universe of the novel, Clarissa's "own information" doesn't have any authority. Her every word is devalued by the female body from which it issues. Although she has, as Anna says at Clarissa's death, "a neat hand, impeccable orthography, [a] simple prose style" (L 529, pp. 1465–72), none of her eloquent letters

---

[23]Richardson, *Clarissa*, p. 40. All future page numbers will be in parentheses in the text. All emphases are Richardson's.

gets her any power in the world. To her family she is "Miss Cunning-ones," and her fluency is simply a sign of her treacherous female tactics. The content of her letters is irrelevant; the mere fact that she writes them shows that she is an unnatural daughter and, finally, an unnatural woman. John Traugott accuses Anna Howe of being "pedestrian [and] irrelevant" "*Clarissa*'s Richardson," (205–6) when she refers to Clarissa's writing style in her eulogy, but the point is precisely that Clarissa's mastery of the tools of rational discourse made her a transgressive and frightening and thus unwomanly creature. Clarissa's sister Arabella writes that her father is afraid that "of writing to so ready a scribbler there will be no end" (L 61, p. 257), and her brother complains that Clarissa is "continually emptying [her] whole female quiver" upon him (L 42.1, p. 198). And, as Clarissa reports to Anna, Arabella is also the messenger for the official, patriarchal interpretation of Clarissa's pleas:

> [She said:] That I next-to-bewitched people, by my insinuating address: that nobody could be valued or respected but must stand like cyphers wherever I came. . . . Specious little witch! she called me: your best manner, so full of art and design, had never been seen through, if you with your blandishing ways had not been put out of sight, and reduced to positive declarations!—hindered from playing your little, whining tricks; curling like a serpent about your mama; and making her cry to deny you anything your little obstinate heart was set upon! (L 42, pp. 194–95)

Clearly, Clarissa's body makes her speech dangerous; it gives to her otherwise transparent language a cunning female power. Clarissa denies that she ever relied on this seductive and duplicitous power—"my mind is above art" (L 42, p. 194)—but the ineffectualness of her epistolary outpourings reveals that her words alone are incapable of carrying the force of the carefully crafted arguments in which she has placed her faith. Clarissa keeps searching for the rhetoric that will convince her father or her uncles or even her brother that she shouldn't have to marry Solmes. She even attacks Solmes as one who has not mastered the language: "Dear, dear sir, if I am to be compelled, let it be in favor of a man that can read and write" (L 32.3, p. 151).

But Clarissa's own words acquire value only after her death. And, of course, her most effective "speech" is the decorated casket itself, proof that the treacherous female body is now safely contained. When she sees the coffin, Anna Howe repeats several times, "And is this all!—is it all of my CLARISSA'S story!" (L 502, p. 1402). There is more to Clarissa's story—the novel we have been reading. But in that novel her story is also surrounded by a kind of triple casket of male interpretation: Lovelace's evil appropriations and forgeries, Belford's benign posthumous collection, and Richardson's omniscient editorial apparatus. Indeed, her original female voice is Richardson's fiction as well—a complication to which I will return.

Even if it is doomed to be misinterpreted, Clarissa's "own information" is all she has. As Anna points out, her "directors and directresses" are all in one way or another untrustworthy. Her mother, for example, "admirably well qualified as she is to lead, must submit to be led." Significantly, Anna doesn't identify the compulsion behind the "must" or the authority to which Mrs. Howe is submitting. We assume it is Mr. Harlowe, but since he is largely absent, we can never be sure. Nor can Clarissa be sure that her brother James, who represents himself as his father's agent, truly speaks for her father.

Yet precisely because he is absent, the characters in Clarissa defer to Mr. Harlowe's absolute authority. He is unknowable and unreachable, the patriarchal equivalent of the correspondent whose physical absence motivates the writing of a letter. And Clarissa, who believes most fervently in his power, keeps writing to him even while they occupy the same house. He refuses to read those letters—he cannot even bear to read her casket. In fact, he almost never responds to anyone directly. Yet his entire family is terrified of him, and that fear causes a fairly simple dispute over marriage plans to escalate speedily into a fight to the death. Tellingly, Lovelace, who sets himself up as a substitute authority, gives the clearest exposition of how Clarissa is crippled by her fantasy that her father will hear her if she finds the proper words: "Yet there are people, and I have talked with some of them, who remember that she was born. . . . But here's her mistake; nor will she be cured of it—she takes the man she calls her father . . . to be her father, . . . and that as such, she owes to [him . . .] reverence [and] respect, let [him] treat her ever so cruelly!" (L 31, p. 145).

For Lovelace, Clarissa's first flaw is that she was born a woman. Her second is her belief that the same hierarchy of gender that makes being born a woman a flaw will protect her. She fails to see that her father's power depends on his absence and that her demands for a hearing thus threaten to topple him from his powerful position. That same paradoxically powerful absence provides the engine for *Clarissa*'s plot. Richardson might be writing of how Mr. Harlowe became powerful through abdication when he explicates to Sophia Westcomb the crucial absence that lends power to the letter. He praises "the pen . . . which makes even presence but body, while absence becomes the soul" (Carroll, 65). Mr. Harlowe's effective abdication allows James and Lovelace, among others, to exercise their authority in his name. And Clarissa, who insists that all men other than her father are mere imposters to patriarchal authority, refuses to bow to these substitutes. Thus the epistolary battle is joined over an authority whose existence can only be surmised from the urgency with which its lack is felt.

Anna Howe, who lives in a matriarchy, is clearsighted about Clarissa's battles with her siblings over the interpretation of their father's will. She concludes her request for Clarissa's version of events with the observation that, "Your sister and brother will certainly put you out of your course." Both of them already hate Clarissa for the preferment her grandfather has shown in bequeathing her an estate in her own name. Her correspondence with Lovelace provides a further excuse for their resentment: he has bested James in a duel and tricked Arabella into refusing his addresses after he'd mistakenly been introduced to her instead of to Clarissa. In the novel's terms, each of these disputes is really a dispute over gender definitions and the proper behavior for men and women. For example, in a patriarchal society Clarissa is not supposed to have a name of her own or the economic independence that assuming her estate would give her. And James has shown himself to be less than a man in his cowardly behavior to Lovelace, and Arabella less than a woman in her failure to attract him. Clarissa doesn't really aspire to a name of her own—she wants her father's name. She shows how deeply she wants the protection of her father's code of gender when she refuses to assume her estate: doing so would free her from her father's power over her, but it would also entail renouncing any claim to his protection or his love. She would be stepping outside of the same hierarchy of gender that has elevated her above all her sex. When she condemns her sister for siding with the oppressor, she reveals her understanding of the irrevocable opposition that hierarchy implies:

> *Female* accents I could distinguish the drowned ones to be. Oh my dear! what a hard-hearted sex is the other! . . . Yet my sister too is as hard-hearted as any of them. But this may be no exception neither: for she has been thought to be masculine in her air, and in her spirit. She has then, perhaps, a soul of the *other* sex in a body of *ours*. And so, for the honour of *our own*, will I judge of every woman for the future who, imitating the rougher manners of men, acts unbeseeming the gentleness of her own sex. (L 79, pp. 309–10)

If Arabella doesn't act like a proper woman, then she is no woman. This is the same kind of reasoning by which Clarissa is declared an unnatural woman when she refuses to marry Solmes. Yet, in a society in which women's writing is suspect because, as Lovelace says, "we have held that women have no souls" (L 220, p. 704), Clarissa wants to be a woman who writes like a man. She is, in the novel's terms, trying to master a tricky balancing act not unlike that required by transvestism. As Anna Howe posthumously reports, she thinks that the "pen, next to the needs, of all employments is the most proper," and she exhorts her sex to "seek to make themselves mistresses of all that is excellent and not incongruous to their sex in the other, but without losing anything commendable in their own" (L 529, pp. 1467–68).

In their different ways, each of *Clarissa*'s characters stumbles over this seemingly unresolvable question of whether or not a woman who writes can be a real woman. And for every character the issue is whether or not the language or the text can be separated from the female body. The Harlowe men, to whom Clarissa is a kind of commodity, useful for trading in exchange for land, try to silence her by depriving her of pen and ink. Clarissa rightly sees this as a violation of her body: "I will now inform you of all that happened previous to their taking away my pen and ink, as well as of the manner in which that act of violence, as I may call it, was committed" (L 79, p. 321).

Mrs. Harlowe, who finds her own puppet status exposed by Clarissa's demands, offers oblique threats about reducing Clarissa to the state she herself has so meekly accepted: "I am loath to interrupt *you*, Clary, though you could more than once break in upon me—You are young and unbroken" (L 17, p. 95).

Lovelace tries to prove that Clarissa, like all other women, is in the end only a body. He fantasizes about impregnating her and seeing "a twin Lovelace at each charming breast" (L 220, p. 706), and he howls in rage when he discovers that his rape has backfired and his seed has taken root in her language instead. That seed prompts her to fool him with her famous allegorical letter misdirecting him to her "father's house" (L 421.1, p. 1233).

Belford, however, attempts to resolve the issue by seeing Clarissa as all mind—by fantasizing that he could free her from the pollution of her woman's body:

She is, in my eye, all mind: and were she to meet with a man all mind likewise, why should the charming qualities she is mistress of, be endangered? Why should such an angel be plunged so low as into the vulgar offices of domestic life? Were she mine, I should hardly wish to see her a mother unless there were a kind of moral certainty that minds like hers could be propagated. For why, in short, should not the work of bodies be left to mere bodies? (L 168, p. 555)

But Lovelace seduces Clarissa by implying that she need not choose between mind and body, language and womanhood. He seems to value her writing as woman's writing. And Clarissa, who is fascinated, is also fully aware of the dangers of writing to a man who recognizes her as a woman. Although she began the correspondence with her mother's implied consent, she sees it as an act of transgression, which makes her fair game for Lovelace's stratagems: "For my own part, I am very uneasy to think how I have been drawn on one hand, and driven on the other, into a clandestine, in short, into a mere lover-like correspondence, which my heart condemns" (L 22, p. 117).

She nevertheless continues to write to Lovelace because he seems eager to read what she has written. He flatters her with his attention to her version of events, and he reinterprets for her the behavior of her family. Thus Lovelace knowingly insinuates himself into the position of authority abdicated by Clarissa's father. Most of all, as a man who loves to write, he seems to offer support for Clarissa's most cherished belief: that writing is an adequate substitute for all of the worldly activities by which men create and express a self. But as Anna Howe points out, Lovelace's fondness for writing in itself should make Clarissa suspicious.

> Our employments are domestic and sedentary, and we can scribble upon twenty innocent subjects and take delight in them because they *are* innocent; though were they to be seen, they might not much profit or please others. But that such a gay, lively young fellow as this, who rides, hunts, travels, frequents the public entertainments, and has *means* to pursue his pleasures, should be able to set himself down to write for hours together, as you and I have heard him say he frequently does, that is the strange thing. (L 12, p. 75)

For a man, Lovelace writes too much and enjoys it too much. This activity, as defined by the novel (and by much Richardson criticism that has so scorned the novelist's prolixity), is suspiciously womanish. What is he doing engaging in the pale imitation that is writing when he could act instead? One or two rakish notes would be permissible as part of the arsenal of seduction, but Lovelace too clearly enjoys wielding the pen, which is, after all, only a substitute for the penis.

Clarissa herself is suspicious (although not suspicious enough) of Lovelace's rhetoric. She can't help but know that words have a different value for him than they do for her. She believes that words have an absolute meaning and must be carefully written and carefully read. She attempts to shepherd her words even after they have left her pen, even attempting to impose a kind of discipline upon her readers: "I lay down my pen here, that you may consider of it a little, if you please" (L 40, p. 186). Lovelace, however, is so confident of what language can do for him that he can afford to play with it. And Clarissa recognizes in his fluency and his playfulness a threat to her own attempts to define herself through language: "I have not the better opinion of Mr. Lovelace for his extravagant volubility. He is too full of professions: he says too many things of me, and to me: True respect, true value, I think, lies not in words: words cannot express it" (L 98, p. 397).

Clarissa's attempts to marshal both the legalistic precision and the worldly power of the patriarch's language prompt Terry Eagleton to assert that Clarissa is a man in writing, and Lovelace a woman.

> The paradox of *Clarissa* is that Clarissa's writing is "masculine" whereas Lovelace's is "feminine". It has been claimed that men and women under patriarchy relate differently to the act of writing. Men, more deeply marked by the "transcendental signifier" of the phallus, will tend to view signs as stable and whole, ideal entities external to the body; women will tend to live a more inward, bodily relationship to script. . . . Clarissa herself exerts the fullest possible control over her meanings, sustaining an enviable coherence of sense even through her worst trials. [Her] relationship to writing is dominative and instrumental. Lovelace, by

contrast, lives on the interior of his prose, generating a provisional identity from the folds of his text, luxuriating in multiple modes of being.[24]

While the seeming opposition between "masculine" and "feminine" writing is crucial to the action of *Clarissa*, however, that opposition clearly exists in order to be complicated. Clarissa's writing is indeed often "masculine"—some of the letters she writes when she is most in despair read like unemotional legal briefs. But her legalistic prose doesn't make Clarissa masculine; it makes her a woman who (seeing in her mother a clear example of the ineffectualness of "feminine" speech or writing) is trying to master the language of the oppressor. Eagleton further neglects to note that her attempt is a failure: even such consummate "masculine" writing is ineffectual when it comes from Clarissa's pen. Similarly, Lovelace does "luxuriat[e] in multiple modes of being," but unlike Clarissa, he can choose to throw off his masquerades at any moment, to reassume the prerogatives of "masculine" speech. He is protean in writing precisely because he is not a woman and so not defined by his body; no language is unsuitable for a man. This latent "masculine" power makes the "feminine" mode valuable to Lovelace in a way it could never be to Clarissa, who would be confined by it.

Thus the paradox of *Clarissa* is not that Clarissa's writing is "masculine" and Lovelace's is "feminine" but that in this novel in which people's lives are destroyed when they transgress the code of proper gendered deportment, the most valued and effective narrative is the transvestite one: Lovelace the great rake borrows feminine modes of being; Belford finds moral salvation by editing—and thus giving legitimacy to—the letters that went unread when Clarissa wrote them to save her own life; and Richardson, through narrative transvestism, creates the woman who—because she is ultimately silenced—can speak for him. And the great irony of Richardson's appropriation of the female voice is that his secure knowledge that he can return to his male,

[24]Eagleton, *Rape of Clarissa*, pp. 52–53.

editorial voice allows him to portray the inevitable result—silence—of Clarissa's struggle to master a language that is antithetical to female being. Simply put, he can speak for Clarissa
precisely because he is not a woman. When "she" is silenced,
"he" can continue to narrate her story.[25]

Lovelace, whose position in the novel is often analogous to
Richardson's authorial stance, defines himself as all that woman
is not; she is that gross material other whose difference affirms
his own mastery over his body and his fate. His letters to Belford
make quite explicit the challenge that Clarissa poses to the concept of woman against which he defines himself. He first claims
that his pursuit of her is simply motivated by the rake's creed,
"Such a triumph over the whole sex, if I can subdue this lady!" (L
103, p. 413). But as he records their complex entanglement, he
acknowledges that he is struggling with Clarissa over the right to
a self and, most immediately, over the control of the self-creating
pen.

> While I was meditating a simple robbery, here have I (in my own
> defence indeed) been guilty of Murder! A bloody murder!—So I
> believe it will prove—At her last gasp!—Poor impertinent op-
> poser! Eternally resisting!—Eternally contradicting! There she lies,
> weltering in her blood! Her death's wound have I given her!—But
> she was a thief, an imposter, as well as a tormentor. She had stolen
> my pen. While I was sullenly meditating, doubting as to my future
> measure, she stole it; and thus she wrote with it, in a hand exactly
> like my own; and would have faced me down, that it was really my
> own handwriting. (L 246, pp. 847–48)

Lovelace's outrage is both genuine and disingenuous: disingenuous because he long ago stole Clarissa's pen in order to
forge letters from Anna Howe to her, and her replies to those
letters; genuine because a woman's attempt to appropriate a

[25]For an attempt by a woman to pursue this same topic, see Mary Wollstonecraft,
Maria, or The Wrongs of Woman (1798; New York: W. W. Norton, 1975), in which the
book itself is fragmented by its female narrator's struggle to find a voice in which a
woman could tell her own story. Unlike Richardson, Wollstonecraft does not have
the overarching structure, and the safe refuge, provided by narrative transvestism.

man's strategy is an insult to the established hierarchy of literary transvestism. Lovelace brags to Belford about how easily he impersonates Anna and Clarissa. Yet the very facility with which he adopts a woman's voice prompts him paradoxically to feel taken over by woman's language. Of his fondness for ever more complicated strategies he writes, "Such a joy when any roguery is going forward!—I so little its master!" (L 153, p. 520). Similarly, he says of his ready interpretation and impersonation of women, "These women think that all the business of the world must stand still for their *figaries* (a good female word, Jack!) . . . (thou seest how women, and women's words, fill my mind)" (L 242, p. 818). He relies on the power that knowing women, or passing for a woman, gets him, but he worries about being polluted by women.

The image of woman to which he customarily refers, however, proves to be inadequate for his conquest of Clarissa. His failure prompts him to assert from time to time that Clarissa is not a woman. She has too much courage and integrity to be the mere disorganized body of his fantasy. And if she is not a mere woman, then she must be, in his terms, either an angel or a man. He toys with the idea that she is somehow both—something of a spiritual transvestite. "And yet, had she not been known to be female, they would not from babyhood have dressed her as such, nor would she, but upon that conviction, have continued the dress" (L 199, p. 642). A few pages later he continues:

> Yet what a contradiction! *Weakness of heart,* says she, with such a *strength of will!*—Oh, Belford! she is a lion-hearted lady in every case where her honour, her punctilio rather, calls for spirit. . . . Yet her charming body is not equally organized. The unequal partners pull two ways; and the divinity within her tears her silken frame. But had the same soul informed a masculine body, never would there have been a truer hero. (L 201, p. 647)

She is too much like him, and for a woman to be like a man is a challenge to the man's power: "Why will she, by her pride, awaken *mine?*" (L 103, p. 413). Even as he asserts that she is powerless, he believes that Clarissa provokes everything he does to her; by refusing to conform to his image of womanhood, she makes him rape her. In fact, he comes to feel that he has been her victim. He writes to Belford of how hard the consequences of the rape have been for him: "But these high-souled and high-sensed girls, who had set up for shining lights and examples to the rest of the sex (I now see that such there are!) are with such difficulty brought down to the common standard, that a wise man, who prefers his peace of mind to his glory in subduing one of that exalted class, would have nothing to say to them" (L 261, p. 889). But Lovelace doesn't prefer peace of mind to glory. He aspires to the position of the transvestite, which he sees as a privileged and desirable one, and to achieve it he needs to possess the most perfect woman he can find. He often fantasizes, for example, about masquerading as a woman to gain access to womanly secrets, and he wants to see Clarissa's reflection when he looks into a mirror.[26] He even explains his success as a rake by comparing himself to Tiresias:

> But I was *originally* a bashful whelp—bashful still, with regard to this lady!—bashful, yet know the sex so well!—But that indeed is the reason that I know it so well—for, Jack, I have had abundant cause, when I have looked into *myself*, by way of comparison with the *other* sex, to conclude that a bashful man has a good deal of the soul of a woman; and so, like Tiresias, can tell what they think and what they drive at, as well as themselves. (L 115, pp. 440–41)

Being a kind of Tiresias is a sign of Lovelace's power; from Clarissa the attempt to reach the same perspective is monstrous.

[26]"Yet, were it so, and life to be the forfeiture of being found at the female churches, I believe I should, like a second Clodius, change by dress to come at any Portia or Calpurnia, though one the daughter of a Cato, the other the wife of a Caesar" (L 106, pp. 419–20). Clodius was a patrician demagogue from the Claudian gens who transformed himself into a plebian and was tried for masquerading as a woman at the festival of the Bona Dea, a Roman goddess worshipped exclusively by women. On the mingling of Lovelace's reflection with Clarissa's: "The glass she dressed at I was ready to break, for not giving me the personal image it was wont to reflect, of *her*, whose idea is for ever present with me (740).

The difference, as always, is that women cannot transcend the confines of their material selves. And Lovelace further makes explicit the equation between a woman's transgressive writing and her always vulnerable body when he intrudes his accusing phallic indices into the margins of a letter he has intercepted from Anna Howe (L 229.1). Similarly, the entire time Clarissa is physically his captive he effectively edits her correspondence, and even after her death he expects his desires to supersede what she has written in her will: "Although her will may in some respects cross mine, yet I expect to be observed. I will be the interpreter of hers" (L 497, p. 1385).

Clarissa certainly asserts that the female letter or text has a body which can be violated, or appropriated, but the novel's most powerful lesson is the other half of the equation: the female body is a text that, if it is to generate meaning, must submit to male intervention and interpretation. Thus, as Clarissa becomes more necessary to him, "the only subject worth writing upon, [without whom] my whole soul is a blank" (L 321, p. 1023), Lovelace has an ever greater need to categorize her: "She cannot bear to be thought a *woman*, I warrant!—and if, in the last attempt, I find her *not* one [. . .]" (L 253, p. 868). And the more steadfastly Clarissa resists Lovelace's reading of her, the more he needs to rape her, to turn her into the passive progenitor of endless numbers of suckling Lovelaces, a speechless body ripe for his own interpretive frenzies. To be a speechless body is her inescapable fate as a woman. Immediately after the rape, Lovelace writes to Belford, "and, when all's done, Miss Clarissa Harlowe has but run the fate of a thousand others of her sex" (L 259, p. 885). He is sure his crime will be redeemed if she is pregnant by him. If she gives bodily expression to his interpretation of her, then the proper hierarchy of gender will have been reestablished. He refers to this as "the charming, charming consequence" (L 268, p. 916) of the rape.

The immediate impact of the rape, however, is to disorganize Clarissa's rhetoric. As her "mad papers" demonstrate, she has temporarily abandoned what Eagleton in *The Rape of Clarissa* calls her "dominative and instrumental" relationship to language. For the first time she writes fiction and poetry; she addresses an unspecified audience, and unlike Belford's description of her as one who "hardly ever stopped or hesitated; and very seldom blotted out or altered" (L 486, p. 1368), she crosses out or tears up what she has written. This woman, for whom language formerly held out the only hope of presenting a unified self to the world, has become rhetorically protean. She experiences her new state as an instability of meanings, "but long have my ears been accustomed to such inversion of words" (L 281, p. 951). She herself is "no longer what [she] was in any one thing" (L 261, p. 890), and Mrs. Sinclair's mannish airs are now cause for doubting "if she be a woman" (L 261.1, p. 894). Nevertheless, she continues to resist Lovelace's attempts to capitalize on the rape; this resistance prompts him to suspect that he has not really penetrated her and that she is not a woman after all. "Against all my notions, against all my conceptions (thinking of her as a woman, and in the very bloom of her charms), she is absolutely invincible!" (L 264, p. 906).

She does, in fact, refuse to submit to the confines of Lovelace's definition of woman, but the rape has destroyed her illusion that she can speak for herself. Recognizing that those who could do so will not speak out for the fallen woman she has become, Clarissa chooses a Christian martyr's death, which allows her story to live on through Belford's and Richardson's editorial intervention. She warns Lovelace: "Make *sure* work, I charge thee: dig a hole deep enough to cram in and conceal this unhappy body: for, depend upon it, that some of those who will not stir to protect me living, will move heaven and earth to avenge me dead!" (L 266, p. 911). They will avenge her when she's dead precisely because they can then ignore the "unhappy body" which defined her life. In her death, Clarissa becomes a purified, bodiless emblem for proper womanhood. Conventional wisdom asserts that because she chooses the manner of it, Clarissa's death is a kind of victory for her. After all, this is the only scene of her life that Clarissa directs. Both her death and the manner of it, however, are dictated by the mechanism of narrative transvestism. Richardson is withdrawing from, and thus silencing, the female narrator he created. Her whole reason for being has always been, after all, to allow him to return to himself. Thus her death is the working out, on the level of the plot, of the inevitable movement away from the female body of the text, back to his reassuringly male editorial stance. Fittingly, Clarissa achieves the peace she seeks by "borrowing" Lovelace's own rhetoric, revealing that theirs is actually the same voice—Richardson's. She tricks Lovelace, as he has so often tricked her, by writing a letter that is literally false and metaphorically true: "Sir, I have good news to tell you. I am setting out with all diligence for my father's house. . . . So, pray, sir, don't disturb or interrupt me—I beseech you don't—You may in time, possibly see me at my father's, at least, if it be not your own fault" (L 421.1, p. 1233).

Thus, in a nice twist on Lovelace's persistent fantasies of "the charming little boys and girls that will be the fruits of this happy reconciliation" (L 421, p. 1234), Clarissa has produced his rhetorical child, which he significantly fails to recognize.

Even with the evidence of the trick before him, however, Lovelace refuses to abandon the fantasy that he can possess this woman if only he possesses her body. To the last he mistakes the body for the whole woman and in a wonderful turn on the metaphor of capturing a true love's heart, he wants to see her embalmed: "But her heart . . . I will have. I will keep it in spirits" (L 497, p. 1384).

By this point in the novel, however, Lovelace is no longer so directly Richardson's stand-in. His is the voice of a particular stage in the process of narrative transvestism—of the man who is inextricably entangled with the woman he is creating and becoming. When Richardson withdraws to his more detached (and therefore less complicatedly male) editorial stance, he leaves Lovelace behind with Clarissa. Those two provisional selves (and provisional genders) really can't be untangled and so—back to the level of plot—they both die. The novel's ending neatly unravels its own narrative and editorial layers, each with its particular gendered valence: Clarissa's last word is her will, or perhaps her coffin; Lovelace's is "LET THIS EXPIATE"; Belford writes the "Conclusion"; and Richardson appends the "Post-script," which instructs us on how to read all the other endings. As always, there are either too many authorities or none at all.

Clarissa's conflict over authoritative speech has its roots in Richardson's discovery of his own authorial power in the devalued unauthoritative female voice of intimacy and helplessness. He plays out the risks involved in his transvestite narrative when he anxiously exercises his editorial (and, in his view, male) control over the unstructured imaginative (and female) realm. He thematizes all sides of the conflict, and all of the stages of transvestism, in the voices and concerns of his fictional letter writers. And in the end he returns, newly strengthened, to the male perspective: Clarissa is finally an "Example to her Sex" (Carroll, 90), not because she preserves her integrity, but because meeting her converts the immoral Belford into a pious gentleman. Through her he learns to become a proper man. He also becomes an editor, of course, rather like Richardson himself. Clarissa's death also teaches women how to be women: it prompts Anna Howe to abandon her efforts to achieve an independent voice and to marry Hickman. Thus Richardson's novel provides a model by which men can learn to read women, and women can learn to allow themselves to be read.

But the novel's impact on its readers is not finally so unambiguous. Central to all of the questions posed by the novel is Richardson's habit of finding his voice by hiding or temporarily suspending his self. He defines parts of his text as female or male, fiction or reality, and letter or editorial comment, and he shuttles back and forth between them. This narrative movement between his female first-person narrator and Lovelace's or Belford's (or the shadowy meta-editor's) interpretations of that woman's story motivates the search within *Clarissa* for an unambiguously gendered authoritative voice. But the novel never finds such a voice; rather, it produces an endlessly suggestive and self-reflexive chorus of voices, all engaged in the creation of a narrative self.

Once more Richardson's letter to his wife, in which he claims to be both a mere pilgrim at the shrine of Clarissa's exemplary death ("May you, my dear Bett, May I . . . benefit . . . by the Examples given in [her history]") and the only true interpreter of her life ("I know so well her Mind"), provides us with a gloss on the artist's skillful disguise of his artistry and on the man's intimate masquerade as a woman. In this suggestive and continual transgression of boundaries, Richardson finds both the voice of intimate confession and the voice of authority. He attempts to provide a similarly unstable but fruitful critical position for his readers by exhibiting his dizzying textual exchange between narrator and editor, man and woman, and author and reader in *Clarissa*. The novel entices and manipulates us and forces us to construct ourselves as "if not Authors, Carpers" in Richardson's divided image.

Conclusion

The preceding pages have presented close readings of two eighteenth-century English novels, Defoe's *Roxana* and Richardson's *Clarissa*. These readings are structured by the concept of narrative transvestism, which directs our attention to the author's exploration of the difficult process of creating a coherent narrative self and to his attempts to engage the reader in that process. I have argued that England's social and political upheaval in the seventeenth century resulted in the early eighteenth century in a reexamination of the categories on which traditional epistemology was based, and in particular in a reexamination of the categories of gender. Both Defoe and Richardson used the device of narrative transvestism to gain access to the uncategorized realm between the genders and to the creative license that accompanied this temporary escape from defining boundaries.

In *Roxana*, Defoe's heroine struggles desperately to escape the constraints of socially defined gender. She attempts to become a "Man-Woman" by accumulating sufficient fortune to maintain her financial independence from men. The only method she has of earning money, however, is prostitution. She is thus trapped by an impossible proposition: she attempts to free herself from the social categories that essentially define women out of existence by marketing herself as the absolute fulfillment of the male fantasy of woman—a "Roxana," or a woman who is whatever a man wants her to be.

The form of Roxana's narrative mirrors her existential dilemma. Its fragmentation expresses the paradox of her narrative endeavor. As a woman she is by definition incoherent. She is trapped within her chaotic experience, and her memoirs are thus another attempt to become a "Man-Woman"—that is, a being whose self could be contained within a coherent narrative. To that end she talks obsessively—driving us to read faster and faster—and several times she promises to reveal the part of her story that will make sense of it all. But she never arrives at that part of her story. Instead, she interrupts herself at every turn with moralizing interpretations of the incompletely related events of her life. And her narrative ceases entirely when she is confronted by a demand for the complete story from within that narrative. Roxana has only been able to talk for so long by refusing to identify with the woman's role that would silence her. Thus it's impossible for her to admit to Susan that she is her mother—that she is at all defined by that woman's role. Her refusal doesn't save her though; she only exchanges the crippling category of woman for the equally crippling one of murderer.

Defoe further uses narrative transvestism to structure his readers' participation in Roxana's dilemma. He plunges us into the flood of Roxana's discourse so that we experience with her the difficulties of creating a coherent life history. And he prompts us to fill the interpretive gap left by her inability to discern a pattern in the events that so confine her. Roxana functions as a receptacle of experience for the reader as well as for Defoe. And, again like Defoe, our distance from that experience allows us to make a coherent whole out of the novel.

Richardson similarly structures his novel around a crucial absence that he entices the reader into filling. By posing as just the printer of the book or Clarissa's "scribbling" amanuensis, he leads us to suspend our awareness of the author outside the text in favor of the authority of the letter writers inside the text. By absenting himself, he heightens the intensity of our reading experience. And by denying that he has invented his characters (a denial which is supported by his habit of quoting from their fictional letters in his personal correspondence), he further involves us in those characters' dilemmas of epistolary self-invention.

Richardson's seeming abdication of his authority as Clarissa's creator is one way he attempts to control our activity as readers. Then, however, he reintroduces himself into the text as an exemplary reader whose interpretations we are meant to follow. In the guises of the internal editor Belford and of the nameless editor who adds footnotes and appendices to the letters, Richardson attempts to preempt any misinterpretive activity by his readers. Thus he never relinquishes his creative authority—he merely disguises it.

On yet another level Richardson draws our attention to his disguise. The plot of *Clarissa* involves so many readers and editors of questionable authority that we come to question Richardson's role as first reader as critically as we would have questioned his admitted authorship of the letters. For just as transvestism destabilizes the categories of gender, although its ultimate goal is to reinforce them, Richardson's temporary transgression of the boundaries between author and reader, or of the outside and the inside of his fictional text, leaves that text vulnerable to just the kinds of intrusive criticism that he sought to forestall. Richardson himself turns us all into not only "Carpers" but "Authors."

Each of these novels contains a character who poses a threat to the transvestite structure of the narrative. In *Roxana*, Susan's demand for facts, for information whose truth or value is not relative, makes her as much a danger to Defoe's delicate narrative balance as she is to Roxana's identity. Yet, as a compelling, unruly and unambiguous figure of femininity, she is also crucial to that narrative—hers is the attractive yet terrifying power to which Defoe seeks access. Similarly, Anna Howe—who is notably not susceptible to Lovelace's charms—is Richardson's figure of a woman who doesn't need a man to define her. Her decision to marry the colorless Hickman is a bow to pragmatism—he will make her life easier in a society bound by strict gender conventions. She does not, however, define herself against him. Unlike Lovelace and Clarissa—or, of course, Richardson himself—she doesn't participate in the transvestite fantasy that Hickman's otherness will lend substantiality to her own being.

Susan and Anna Howe are figures for whom gender identity is not problematic. And precisely because their femininity is not dependent upon an other's masculinity, they are problematic for their authors. For Defoe and Richardson are, of course, caught up in the same transvestite structure that is so enabling but finally so limiting for their heroines. Like their heroines, they depend for their narrative effectiveness on an uneasy alliance of contradictory impulses. And, like real-world transvestites, they must disguise themselves to find themselves.

Both Defoe and Richardson deliberately exploit the contradictions inherent in their use of a female voice to structure their novels' explorations of the relationships of gendered categories to each other. Defoe displays his self-consciousness and his playfulness about the intersection of structure with theme when he has Roxana fulminate against male "Fools," or declare her ambition to be a "Man-Woman," as does Richardson when Lovelace longs to be a new kind of Tiresias or when he and Clarissa seem to exchange gendered characteristics through their letters. Having chosen a structure that risked tumbling their fictions into the undefined chaos between binary poles, both these authors exploited the resulting fissures in their narratives. Those fissures become the gaps through which the reader is enticed—or at times almost coerced—into participating in the narrative project of the novels.

Literary critics who have written about a male author's use of a female voice in literature have often included Cleland's *Memoirs of a Woman of Pleasure* (*Fanny Hill*) in their examples. Cleland's use of a female narrator in *Fanny Hill*, however, does not meet the criteria of the structural device I have called narrative transvestism. A brief look at recent criticism of this novel will serve to

point up the differences between my concept of narrative transvestism and recent critical efforts to characterize the male author's use of a female narrator as either an appropriation or a
privileging of the female voice.

Nancy K. Miller, in the paper that first brought this narrative
device to the attention of many readers, cites *Fanny Hill* as an
example of the use by a male author of an ersatz female voice to
"attain recognition from other men."[1] More recently, Julia Epstein has proposed that Cleland exploits the homoeroticism of
the novel by emphasizing the exchange of the letters between
women (Fanny and her female correspondent). She concludes
by agreeing with Miller that "Cleland in fact imposes a homoerotic phallocentrism on the pleasures his text narrates, with its
apparently heterosexual subject matter and its apparently lesbian formal presentation. By using letters literally to *embody*
Fanny's eternal feminine receptivity, the text thereby dispos-
sesses and expels her."[2]

Certainly, as these critics claim, Cleland appropriates a female
narrative voice for his own, and he uses that supposedly female
voice to extoll the glories of male sexuality and of the male sexual
organ in particular.[3] Yet, although his novel uses both the epistolary and the memoir forms that Defoe and Richardson used to
exploit the ambiguities of narrative transvestism, Cleland's narrative is seamless. It has only one structural division between the
two letters; as a result, the issues that are so crucial to epistolarity—such as the risks in writing to an absent audience whose
willing reception of those letters is in doubt—never come into
play. Similarly, although Fanny begins her career as a prostitute

---

[1] Nancy K. Miller, " 'I's' in Drag," p. 51.

[2] Julia Epstein, "Fanny's Fanny: Epistolarity, Eroticism, and the Transsexual Text,"
in Elizabeth C. Goldsmith ed., *Writing the Female Voice* (Boston: Northeastern University Press, 1989), p. 148.

[3] The real dangers of prostitution never intrude on this utopian fantasy. Randolph
Trumbach has recently emphasized this fantasy element by detailing the grim and
dangerous lives of real prostitutes in "Modern Prostitution and Gender in *Fanny Hill*:
Libertine and Domesticated Fantasy," in Rousseau and Porter, eds., *Sexual Underworlds*, pp. 69–85.

because she misinterprets what her employer is offering her, neither her misinterpretation nor Mother Brown's implicit linguistic tyranny become thematic issues in the novel as they do, for example, in *Clarissa.*

Instead, Fanny condemns her own "invincible stupidity, or rather portentous innocence"[4] and hastens to assure us that "neither virtue or principles had the least share in the defence I had made but only the particular aversion I had conceived against this first brutal and frightful invader of my tender innocence" (59). Fanny is an uncomplicated misogynist—further evidence that Cleland's novel lacks the ambiguities and exchanges of gendered perspectives that are characteristic of narrative transvestism.

Fanny quickly masters the language of her new environment, and neither she nor the reader ever experiences any dislocation between her former wholesome, provincial self and the urban demi-mondaine she has become, or, indeed, between her supposedly female being and the male voice that is speaking through her. Although this is a first-person narrative, Fanny tells us remarkably little about herself. Instead, she turns the same pragmatic eye on every aspect of her experience, and she relates them all in the same dry tone (the excesses of her florid metaphors for the penis notwithstanding), as if they were happening to someone else. For example, when her "benefactress" propels her into her first real service as a prostitute immediately after her night with Charles (the first man she'd ever known, and as it turns out, the only man she ever loved), Fanny prefaces her description of Mr. H's ardor with this comment on her feelings: "Violent passions seldom last long, and those of women least of any" (97). She follows her detailed account of Mr. H's activities with a flat statement of her new status: "I was now established the kept mistress in form, well lodged, with a very sufficient allowance and lighted up with all the lustre of dress" (103).

[4]John Cleland, *Memoirs of a Woman of Pleasure,* ed. Peter Wagner (New York: Penguin, 1985), p. 54. Further page references are in parentheses in the text.

In short, Fanny is even more absent from her experience than is Roxana at her most passive. As a result, Cleland doesn't explore his narrative masquerade anywhere in his novel. He makes no effort to express a woman's perspective, to appropriate her voice, or to share vicariously in her experience. He simply tells us that the letters we're reading were written by a woman, and he ignores the implications of this assertion for the construction and subsequent transgression of gender boundaries in the novel.[5] This absence of any thematic or structural exploitation of the masquerade leads me to conclude that *Fanny Hill* is not an example of a transvestite narrative. Rather, Cleland is doing something much simpler and—to my mind—much less interesting. He has created a pornotopic fantasy of woman who is, in fact, not other at all. Her body, despite its lack of a penis, mirrors in its responses the male model of sexuality. Similarly, the single subject of her monologue is men, and she sees men only as their wildest fantasies portray them. She regards "that wonderful machine" (62), the male penis, with awe and delight. Her primary worry when confronted with a client who wants her to act out his sadistic and masochistic fantasies is that he will scorn her weakness if she hesitates: "I was now less afraid of my skin than of his not furnishing me an opportunity of signalizing my resolution" (185). And, as always in this book, her sexual tastes quickly adapt to his. Although immediately after her

---

[5]In his chapters on *Pamela* and *Fanny Hill*, Roy Roussel, in *The Conversation of the Sexes: Seduction and Equality in Selected Seventeenth- and Eighteenth-Century Texts* (New York: Oxford University Press, 1986), tries to make sense out of the constantly changing positions of male and female in the dyads of the two narratives by recourse to an ideal of androgyny: "Cleland is . . . interested in the way this pleasure elicits a sense of internal play between masculine and feminine which subverts conventional gender identifications. In this way the novel moves toward a certain idea of androgyny in which the equality between masculine and feminine triumphs over the difference between the sexes and allows the man and the woman to converse freely across this difference" (41).

Roussel argues that Mr. B. achieves this androgynous perspective in *Pamela*, and that the (presumably male) reader of *Fanny Hill* resolves the tension generated by the play of genders in this same way. Although he doesn't deal at length with Cleland's use of a female narrator, Roussel would obviously disagree with my assertion that Cleland ignores the implications of his choice.

whipping she is "scarce in charity with my butcher" (187), soon "a change so incredible was wrought in me, such violent yet pleasingly irksome sensations took possession of me that I scarce know how to contain myself" (187).

Indeed, the only men who inspire any critical words from her at all are two homosexuals on whom she spies at an inn. Her scorn is particularly directed at the younger and the more passive of the two men, the "Ganymede" whom she describes as one who "if he was like his mother behind he was like his father before" (195). The confusion of gender roles in this "so criminal a scene" (195) particularly disturbs Fanny, and she accuses "these unsexed male misses" (196) of the worst fault she can imagine— that of sacrificing their pure and noble masculinity to be more like women. They are "stripped of all the manly virtues of their own sex and filled up with only the very worst vices and follies of ours" (196). Still, she feels compelled to remind us that women are even worse, and she plunges immediately into a story designed to be "confirmation of the maxim that when women get once out of compass, there are no lengths of licentiousness they are not capable of running" (196–97).

Such a scene in a novel by Defoe or Richardson would be an occasion to explore the complications of narrative transvestism and the absurd mirroring of their narrative selves in this creature who is "like his mother behind" and "his father before." But Cleland is not interested in the implications of his narrative choices or in redefining the realms that narrative can explore by adopting a destabilizing structure. In fact, despite its pornographic subject, *Fanny Hill* is a deeply conservative model. It works best as a straightforward conduct book, intended for an audience of apt women pupils along with its more obvious audience of titillated men. Fanny's story of how she came to be a fulfilled woman is Cleland's attempt to educate women to be the uncomplaining and uncomplicated sexual toys that they were in his fantasy. And, like Richardson's *Pamela*, *Fanny Hill* holds out the prospect of marital happiness and material wealth to its properly educated heroine. Such a reading puts a new spin on Cleland's claim that his novel was not intended as pornography: despite its daring subject matter, it was intended to uphold the patriarchal and bourgeois system in which women who "have served . . . as looking-glasses possessing the magic and delicious power of reflecting the figure of man at twice its natural size"[6] are rewarded with the legitimization of their existence that men could offer through marriage.

In contrast to *Fanny Hill*, the authorial presence in *Roxana* and in *Clarissa* is, as I have shown, ambiguous and extremely complicated. For example, when we pursue the vertiginous layers of men speaking for women speaking for men speaking for women that we can find in Richardson's portrayal of Lovelace's forgery of Anna Howe's letters and of Clarissa's replies to them, we find ourselves on the brink of an abyss in which it is hard to locate the author and it is difficult to distinguish the truths of masks from the truths of the unmasked.

Thus the transgression of the boundaries between genders in narrative transvestism extends to the transgression of an entire binary epistemological structure. And the novel is revealed as a paradoxical and hence destabilizing genre which finds its form in formlessness, just as Defoe and Richardson found their voices by seeming to silence themselves. In a period that longed for the balance and stability that binary structures seemed to offer, the novel emerged as a form designed for the exploration of the undefined realm between the poles. The early novelists' use of narrative transvestism allowed them to develop a structure that both fostered and protected such exploration. This new fictional form was thus revolutionary and yet very much a participant in the literary and cultural mainstream of eighteenth-century England. We can recognize Swift's, Johnson's, Pope's, or even Addison's themes and concerns in the novel, and yet in the novel, old systems, old relationships, and old structures have been

[6]Virginia Woolf, *A Room of One's Own* (New York: Harcourt Brace, 1929), p. 35.

turned inside out. The transvestite narrative speaks from between the poles, mapping that always necessary but formerly unacknowledged territory and suggestively transgressing the boundaries that are no longer so comfortably impermeable.

We might say, as Johnson did of Pope, that the early novelists "extracted an ornament from an inconvenience."[7] Defoe and Richardson embraced the confusion of genders as both form and theme, and they turned the novel inward to private experience and the individual's efforts to define a self. Thus the novelist's artistic task and the individual's existential one mirror each other, and reader and author together resolve the chaos and ambiguities of efforts at self-definition into a temporary formal unity.

[7]Johnson, "Life of Pope," p. 135.

Selected Bibliography

Abel, Elizabeth, ed. *Writing and Sexual Difference*. Chicago: University of Chicago Press, 1982.

Ackroyd, Peter. *Dressing Up: Transvestism and Drag, the History of an Obsession*. New York: Simon and Schuster, 1979.

Altman, Janet. *Epistolarity: Approaches to a Form*. Columbus: Ohio State University Press, 1982.

Ariès, Phillippe, and André Béjin, eds. *Western Sexuality: Practice and Precept in Past and Present Times*. London: Basil Blackwell, 1985.

Armstrong, Nancy. *Desire and Domestic Fiction: A Political History of the Novel*. New York: Oxford University Press, 1987.

Ashton, John. *Eighteenth Century Waifs*. 1887. Freeport, N.Y.: Books for Libraries Press, 1972.

Babcock, Barbara, ed. *The Reversible World: Symbolic Inversion in Art and Society*. Ithaca: Cornell University Press, 1978.

Backscheider, Paula. *A Being More Intense: A Study of the Prose Works of Bunyan, Swift, and Defoe*. New York: AMS Press, 1984.

——. *Daniel Defoe: Ambition and Innovation*. Lexington: University of Kentucky Press, 1986.

Bakhtin, M. M. *The Dialogic Imagination: Four Essays*. Ed. Michael Holquist. Trans. Caryl Emerson and Michael Holquist. Austin: University of Texas Press, 1981.

——. *Rabelais and His World*. Trans. Helene Iswolsky. Cambridge: MIT Press, 1968.

Ballard, George. *Memoirs of Several Ladies of Great Britain*. Ed. Ruth Perry. Detroit: Wayne State University Press, 1985.

Barthes, Roland. *S/Z*. Trans. Richard Miller. New York: Farrar, Straus, and Giroux, 1974.

Beauvoir, Simone de. *The Second Sex*. 1952. Ed. and trans. H. M. Parshley. New York: Vintage Books, 1974.

Bell, Quentin. *On Human Finery*. New York: Schocken Books, 1976.
Bell, Susan Groag, and Karen M. Offen. *Women, the Family, and Freedom: The Debate in Documents*. Vol. 1, *1750–1880*. Stanford: Stanford University Press, 1983.
Bender, John. *Imagining the Penitentiary: Fiction and the Architecture of Mind in Eighteenth-Century England*. Chicago: University of Chicago Press, 1987.
——. "The Novel and the Rise of the Penitentiary: Narrative and Ideology in Defoe, Gay, Hogarth, and Fielding." *Stanford Literature Review* 1 (Spring 1984): 55–84.
Benjamin, Jessica. "A Desire of One's Own: Psychoanalytic Feminism and Intersubjective Space." In *Feminist Studies/Critical Studies*. Ed. Teresa de Lauretis, 78–101. Bloomington: Indiana University Press, 1986.
Benveniste, Emile. *Problems in General Linguistics*. Trans. Mary Elizabeth Meek. Coral Gables: University of Miami Press, 1971.
Berguin, Victor, ed. *Formations of Fantasy*. New York: Methuen, 1986.
Bernheimer, Charles, and Claire Kahane, eds. *In Dora's Case: Freud-Hysteria-Feminism*. New York: Columbia University Press, 1985.
Bettelheim, Bruno. *Symbolic Wounds, Puberty Rites, and the Envious Male*. Glencoe, Ill.: Free Press, 1954.
Blewett, David. *Defoe's Art of Fiction: Robinson Crusoe, Moll Flanders, Colonel Jack, and Roxana*. Toronto: University of Toronto Press, 1979.
Bloch, Ivan. *A History of English Sexual Morals*. Trans. William H. Forstern. London: Francis Aldor, 1936.
Boswell, James. *Life of Samuel Johnson*. Garden City, N.Y.: Doubleday, 1946.
——. *London Journal*. New York: McGraw Hill, 1980.
Boucé, Paul Gabriel, ed. *Sexuality in Eighteenth Century Britain*. Manchester: Manchester University Press, 1982.
Braudy, Leo. "Penetration and Impenetrability in *Clarissa*." In *New Approaches to Eighteenth-Century Literature*. Ed. Phillip Harth, 177–206. New York: Columbia University Press, 1974.
Brooks, Peter. "The Idea of a Psychoanalytic Literary Criticism." *Critical Inquiry* 15 (Winter 1987): 334–48.
Brown, J. Christie. "Paraphilias: Sadomasochism, Fetishism, Transvestism, and Transsexuality." *British Journal of Psychiatry* 143 (September 1983): 227–31.
Brownstein, Rachel Mayer. "An Exemplar to Her Sex: Richardson's *Clarissa*." *Yale Review* 67 (1977): 30–47.
Buhrich, Neil and Neil McConaghy. "Transvestite Fiction." *Journal of Nervous and Mental Disease* 163 (December 1976): 420–27.
Bullough, Vern. "Transvestites in the Middle Ages." *American Journal of Sociology* 79 (1974): 1381–94.
Butler, Judith. *Gender Trouble*. New York: Routledge, 1990.
Caplan, Pat, ed. *The Cultural Construction of Sexuality*. London: Tavistock, 1987.
Carson, James. "Narrative Cross-Dressing and the Critique of Authorship in the Novels of Richardson." In *Writing the Female Voice: Essays on Episto-*

lary Literature. Ed. Elizabeth C. Goldsmith, 95–113. Boston: Northeastern University Press, 1989.

Castle, Terry. "'*Amy*, who knew my Disease': A Psychosexual Pattern in Defoe's *Roxana*." *ELH* (Fall 1979): 81–96.

——— *Clarissa's Ciphers: Meaning and Disruption in Richardson's "Clarissa."* Ithaca: Cornell University Press, 1982.

———. "The Culture of Travesty: Sexuality and Masquerade in Eighteenth-Century England." In *Sexual Underworlds of the Enlightenment*. Ed. G. S. Rousseau and Roy Porter, 156–80. Manchester: Manchester University Press, 1987.

———. *Masquerade and Civilization: The Carnivalesque in Eighteenth-Century English Culture and Fiction*. Stanford: Stanford University Press, 1986.

———. "Matters Not Fit to Be Mentioned: Fielding's *The Female Husband*." *ELH* 49 (Fall 1982): 602–22.

Charke, Charlotte. *A Narrative of the Life of Mrs. Charlotte Charke (Youngest Daughter of Colley Cibber, Esq.), Written by Herself*. Ed. Leonard R. N. Ansley. Gainesville, Fla.: Scholarly Facsimilies & Reprints, 1969.

Chodorow, Nancy. "Feminism and Difference: Gender, Relation, and Difference in Psychoanalytic Perspective." *Socialist Review* 46 (July–August 1979): 51–69.

———. *The Reproduction of Mothering: Psychoanalysis and the Sociology of Gender*. Berkeley: University of California Press, 1978.

Cixous, Hélène. "The Laugh of the Medusa." In *New French Feminisms*. Ed. Elaine Marks and Isabelle de Courtivron, 245–64. New York: Schocken, 1981.

Cleland, John. *Memoirs of a Woman of Pleasure*. Ed. Peter Wagner. New York: Penguin, 1985.

Colie, Rosalie L. *Paradoxia Epidemica: The Renaissance Tradition of Paradox*. Princeton: Princeton University Press, 1966.

Cox, Cynthia. *The Enigma of the Age: The Strange Story of the Chevalier d'Éon*. London: Longman's, 1966.

Damrosch, Leopold, Jr. "Defoe as Ambiguous Impersonator." *Modern Philology* 71 (1973): 153–59.

Davis, Natalie Zemon. *Society and Culture in Early Modern France*. Stanford: Stanford University Press, 1975.

Day, Robert A. *Told in Letters: Epistolary Fiction before Richardson*. Ann Arbor: University of Michigan Press, 1960.

Defoe, Daniel. *The Letters of Daniel Defoe*. Ed. G. H. Healey. Oxford: Clarendon Press, 1955.

———. *Roxana: The Fortunate Mistress*. 1724. Ed. Jane Jack. New York: Oxford University Press, 1981.

Delaney, Sheila. *Writing Woman: Women Writers and Women in Literature, Medieval to Modern*. New York: Schocken Books, 1983.

de Lauretis, Teresa, ed. *Feminist Studies/Critical Studies*. Bloomington: Indiana University Press, 1986.

164   Selected Bibliography

Docter, Richard F. *Transvestites and Transsexuals: Toward a Theory of Cross-Gender Behavior*. New York: Plenum Press, 1988.

Doody, Margaret Anne. *A Natural Passion: A Study of the Novels of Samuel Richardson*. Oxford: Clarendon Press, 1974.

Dugaw, Diane. "Balladry's Female Warriors: Women, Warfare, and Disguise in the Eighteenth Century." *Eighteenth Century Life* 9 (1985): 1–20.

Eagleton, Terry. *Literary Theory: An Introduction*. Minneapolis: University of Minnesota Press, 1983.

———. *The Rape of Clarissa: Writing, Sexuality, and Class Struggle in Samuel Richardson*. Minneapolis: University of Minnesota Press, 1982.

Eaves, T. C. Duncan, and Ben D. Kimpel. *Samuel Richardson: A Biography*. Oxford: Clarendon Press, 1971.

Ehrenpreis, Irvin. "Personae." In *Restoration and Eighteenth-Century Literature: Essays in Honor of Alan Dugald McKillop*. Ed. Carroll Camden, 25–37. Chicago: University of Chicago Press, 1963.

Ellis, Havelock. *Studies in the Psychology of Sex*. Vol. III, Part II, *Eonism and Other Supplementary Studies*. New York: Random House, 1936.

Epstein, Julia. "Fanny's Fanny: Epistolarity, Eroticism, and the Transsexual Text." In *Writing the Female Voice: Essays on Epistolary Literature*. Ed. Elizabeth C. Goldsmith, 135–53. Boston: Northeastern University Press, 1989.

Erickson, Robert A. *Mother Midnight: Birth, Sex, and Fate in Eighteenth-Century Fiction (Defoe, Richardson, and Sterne)*. New York: AMS Press, 1986.

Faderman, Lillian. *Surpassing the Love of Men: Romantic Friendship and Love Between Women from the Renaissance to the Present*. New York: William Morrow, 1981.

Feinbloom, Deborah. *Transvestites and Transsexuals: Mixed Views*. New York: Delacorte Press/Seymour Lawrence, 1975.

Felman, Shoshana, ed. *Literature and Psychoanalysis: The Question of Reading Otherwise*. Baltimore: Johns Hopkins University Press, 1982.

Fenichel, Otto. "The Psychology of Transvestism." *International Journal of Psycho-Analysis* 11 (April 1930): 211–27.

Fielding, Henry. *The Female Husband*. In *The Female Husband and Other Writings*. Ed. Claude E. Jones, 28–51. Liverpool: Liverpool University Press, 1960.

Fielding, Sarah. *Remarks on Clarissa*. 1749. William Andrews Clark Memorial Library. Los Angeles: University of California Press, 1985.

Flugel, J. C. *The Psychology of Clothes*. London: Hogarth Press, 1930.

Flynn, Carol H. *Samuel Richardson: A Man of Letters*. Princeton: Princeton University Press, 1982.

Foster, Jeannette H. *Sex Variant Women in Literature*. New York: Vantage Press, 1956.

Foucault, Michel. *The History of Sexuality*. Vol. I, *An Introduction*. New York: Vintage Books, 1980.

———. Introduction. *Herculine Barbin, Being the Recently Discovered Memoirs of a Nineteenth-Century French Hermaphrodite*. Trans. Richard McDougall. New York: Pantheon, 1980.

Freud, Sigmund. "The Antithetical Sense of Primal Words." 1910. In *Character and Culture*. Ed. Philip Rieff, 44–50. New York: Macmillan, 1963.

———. *Leonardo da Vinci: A Study in Psychosexuality*. Trans. A. A. Brill. New York: Vintage Books, 1916.

———. *Three Essays on the Theory of Sexuality*. 1905. Trans. James Strachey. New York: Avon Books, 1962.

Friedli, Lynn. " 'Passing women'—A Study of Gender Boundaries in the Eighteenth Century." In *Sexual Underworlds of the Enlightenment*. Ed. G. S. Rousseau and Roy Porter, 234–60. Manchester: Manchester University Press, 1987.

Gaillardet, Frederick, ed. *The Memoirs of the Chevalier d'Éon*. Trans. Antonia White. London: Anthony Blond, 1970.

Gallop, Jane. *The Daughter's Seduction: Feminism and Psychoanalysis*. Ithaca: Cornell University Press, 1982.

Garner, Shirley Nelson, Claire Kahane, and Madelon Sprengnether, eds. *The (M)other Tongue: Essays in Feminist Psychoanalytic Interpretation*. Ithaca: Cornell University Press, 1985.

Gilbert, Sandra M., and Susan Gubar. "Costumes of the Mind: Transvestism as Metaphor in Modern Literature." In *Writing and Sexual Difference*. Ed. Elizabeth Abel, 193–220. Chicago: University of Chicago Press, 1982.

———. *The Madwoman in the Attic: The Woman Writer and the Nineteenth-Century Literary Imagination*. New Haven: Yale University Press, 1979.

Goffman, Erving. *The Presentation of Self in Everyday Life*. New York: Doubleday, 1959.

———. *Stigma: Notes on the Management of Spoiled Identity*. Englewood Cliffs, N.J.: Prentice-Hall, 1963.

Goreau, Angeline. "Two English Women in the Seventeenth Century: Notes for an Anatomy of Feminine Desire." In *Western Sexuality: Practice and Precept in Past and Present Times*. Ed. Philippe Ariès and André Béjin, 103–13. Trans. Anthony Forster. Oxford: Basil Blackwell, 1986.

Gosselin, Chris, and Glenn Wilson. *Sexual Variations: Fetishism, Sadomasochism, and Transvestism*. London: Faber and Faber, 1980.

Greenblatt, Stephen. "Fiction and Friction." In *Reconstructing Individualism: Autonomy, Individuality, and the Self in Western Thought*. Ed. Thomas C. Heller, Morton Sosna, and David E. Wellbery, 30–52. Stanford: Stanford University Press, 1986.

Gubar, Susan. "Blessings in Disguise: Cross-Dressing as Re-Dressing for Female Modernists." *Massachusetts Review* 22 (1981): 477–508.

———. "The Female Monster in Augustan Satire." *Signs* 3 (Winter 1977): 380–94.

Hagstrum, Jean H. *Sex and Sensibility: Ideal and Erotic Love from Milton to Mozart*. Chicago: University of Chicago Press, 1980.

Halperin, David. *One Hundred Years of Homosexuality: And Other Essays on Greek Love*. New York: Routledge, 1990.

Hay, Douglas, Peter Linebaugh, John G. Rule, E. P. Thompson, and Cal Winslow. *Albion's Fatal Tree: Crime and Society in Eighteenth-Century England*. New York: Pantheon Books, 1975.

Heath, Stephen. "Joan Rivière and the Masquerade." In *Formations of Fantasy*. Ed. V. Berguin, 45–61. New York: Methuen, 1986.

Heilbrun, Carolyn G. *Toward a Recognition of Androgyny*. New York: Harper and Row, 1973.

Heller, Thomas C., Morton Sosna, and David E. Wellbery, eds. *Reconstructing Individualism: Autonomy, Individuality, and the Self in Western Thought*. With Arnold I. Davidson, Ann Swidler, and Ian Watt. Stanford: Stanford University Press, 1986.

Hill, Christopher. *The World Turned Upside Down: Radical Ideas during the English Revolution*. New York: Penguin, 1972.

Homberg, Octave, ed. *D'Éon de Beaumont: His Life and Times*. Trans. Alfred Rieu. London: Martin Secker, 1911.

Hunter, J. Paul. *The Reluctant Pilgrim: Defoe's Emblematic Method and Quest for Form in Robinson Crusoe*. Baltimore: Johns Hopkins University Press, 1966.

Irigaray, Luce. *This Sex Which Is Not One*. Trans. Catherine Porter, with Carolyn Burke. Ithaca: Cornell University Press, 1985.

Jarret, Derek. *England in the Age of Hogarth*. New York: Viking, 1974.

Jelinek, Estelle C. "Disguise Autobiographies: Women Masquerading as Men." *Women's Studies International Forum* 10.1 (1987): 53–62.

Johnson, Barbara. *The Critical Difference: Essays in the Contemporary Rhetoric of Reading*. Baltimore: Johns Hopkins University Press, 1980.

Johnson, Samuel. "The Life of Pope." In *The Lives of the English Poets*. Ed. George Birbeck Hill, 3: 82–280. Oxford: Clarendon Press, 1935.

Kamuf, Peggy. "Writing Like a Woman." In *Women and Language in Literature and Society*. Ed. Sally McConnell-Ginet, Ruth Borker, and Nelly Furman, 284–99. New York: Praeger, 1980.

Kauffman, Linda S. *Discourses of Desire: Gender, Genre, and Epistolary Fictions*. Ithaca: Cornell University Press, 1986.

Kinkead-Weekes, Mark. *Samuel Richardson: Dramatic Novelist*. Ithaca: Cornell University Press, 1973.

Kreissman, Bernard. *Pamela-Shamela*. Lincoln: University of Nebraska Press, 1960.

Lacan, Jacques. *Écrits: A Selection*. Trans. Alan Sheridan. New York: W. W. Norton, 1977.

Lakoff, Robin. *Language and Woman's Place*. New York: Harper and Row, 1975.

Laqueur, Thomas. "Orgasm, Generation, and the Politics of Reproductive Biology." *Representations* 14 (Spring 1986): 1–41.

LeGates, Marlene. "The Cult of Womanhood in Eighteenth-Century Thought." *Eighteenth Century Studies* 10 (Fall 1976): 21–39.

Levine, Laura. "Men in Women's Clothing: Anti-theatricality and Effeminization from 1579–1642." *Criticism* 28 (Spring 1986): 121–43.

Lloyd, Genevieve. *The Man of Reason, "Male" and "Female" in Western Philosophy*. London: Methuen, 1984.

MacCormack, Carol P., and Marilyn Strathern, eds. *Nature, Culture, and Gender*. Cambridge: Cambridge University Press, 1980.

McKeon, Michael. *The Origins of the English Novel, 1600–1740*. Baltimore: Johns Hopkins University Press, 1987.

McKillop, Allan D. *Samuel Richardson: Printer and Novelist*. Chapel Hill: University of North Carolina Press, 1936.

Marks, Elaine, and Isabelle de Courtivron, eds. *New French Feminisms*. New York: Schocken, 1981.

Marshall, David. *The Figure of Theater: Shaftesbury, Defoe, Adam Smith, and George Eliot*. New York: Columbia University Press, 1986.

Mathieu, Nicole-Claude. *Ignored by Some Denied by Others: The Social Sex Category in Sociology*. London: Women's Research and Resource Centre Publications, 1978.

Mavor, Elizabeth, ed. *A Year with the Ladies of Llangollen*. New York: Penguin, 1986.

Miller, Nancy K. "Emphasis Added: Plots and Plausibilities in Women's Fiction." *PMLA* 96 (January 1981): 36–48.

———. "The Exquisite Cadavers: Women in Eighteenth-Century Fiction." *Diacritics* 5 (Winter 1975): 37–53.

———. *The Heroine's Text: Readings in the French and English Novel, 1722–1782*. New York: Columbia University Press, 1980.

———. " 'I's' in Drag: The Sex of Recollection." *The Eighteenth Century: Theory and Interpretation* 22 (Winter 1981): 47–57.

———. "The Text's Heroine: A Feminist Critic and Her Fictions." *Diacritics* 12 (Summer 1982): 48–53.

———, ed. *The Poetics of Gender*. New York, Columbia University Press, 1986.

Mitchell, Juliet, and Jacqueline Rose, eds. *Feminine Sexuality: Jacques Lacan and the École Freudienne*. London: MacMillan, 1982.

Moore, John Robert. *Daniel Defoe: Citizen of the Modern World*. Chicago: University of Chicago Press, 1958.

Nixon, Edna. *Royal Spy: The Strange Case of the Chevalier d'Éon*. New York: Reynal, 1965.

Novak, Maximillian, ed. *English Literature in the Age of Disguise*. Berkeley: University of California Press, 1977.

Nussbaum, Felicity A. *The Brink of All We Hate: English Satires on Women, 1660–1750*. Lexington: University of Kentucky Press, 1984.

———, and Laura Brown, eds. *The New Eighteenth Century*. New York: Methuen, 1988.

Ober, William. *Boswell's Clap and Other Essays: Medical Analyses of Literary Men's Afflictions*. Carbondale: Southern Illinois University Press, 1979.

———. *Bottoms Up!: A Pathologist's Essays on Medicine and the Humanities*. New York: Harper and Row, 1987.

Ogden, Thomas H. *Projective Identification and Psychotherapeutic Technique*. New York: Jason Aronson, 1982.

Ortner, Sherry B. "Is Female to Male as Nature is to Culture?" *Feminist Studies* 1 (Fall 1972): 5–31.

Ovid, *Metamorphoses*. Trans. Rolfe Humphries. Bloomington: Indiana University Press, 1955.

Perry, Ruth. *The Celebrated Mary Astell: An Early English Feminist.* Chicago: University of Chicago Press, 1986.

——. *Women, Letters, and the Novel.* New York: AMS Press, 1980.

Pollak, Ellen. *The Poetics of Sexual Myth: Gender and Ideology in the Verse of Swift and Pope.* Chicago: University of Chicago Press, 1985.

Poovey, Mary. *The Proper Lady and the Woman Writer: Ideology as Style in the Works of Mary Wollstonecraft, Mary Shelley, and Jane Austen.* Chicago: University of Chicago Press, 1984.

Pope, Alexander. *Poetry and Prose of Alexander Pope.* Ed. Aubrey Williams. Boston: Houghton Mifflin, 1969.

Porter, Roy. *English Society in the Eighteenth Century.* New York: Penguin, 1982.

Quaritch, Bernard. Sale catalogue # 1083. Fall 1987, pp. 36–38.

Redford, Bruce. *The Converse of the Pen: Acts of Intimacy in the Eighteenth-Century Familiar Letter.* Chicago: University of Chicago Press, 1986.

Richardson, Samuel. *Clarissa, or the History of a Young Lady.* Ed. Angus Ross. New York: Penguin, 1985.

——. *The Selected Letters of Samuel Richardson.* Ed. John Carroll. Oxford: Clarendon Press, 1964.

Richetti, John J. *Defoe's Narratives: Situations and Structures.* Oxford: Clarendon Press, 1975.

——. *Popular Fiction before Richardson: Narrative Patterns, 1700–1739.* Oxford: Clarendon Press, 1969.

——. "The Portrayal of Women in Restoration and Eighteenth-Century English Literature." In *What Manner of Woman: Essays on English and American Life and Literature.* Ed. Marlene Springer, 65–97. New York: New York University Press, 1977.

Rivière, Joan. "Womanliness as Masquerade." In *Formations of Fantasy.* Ed. V. Berguin, 35–44. New York: Methuen, 1986.

Rosaldo, Michelle Z., and Louise Lamphere, eds. *Woman, Culture, and Society.* Stanford: Stanford University Press, 1974.

Rousseau, G. S., and Roy Porter, eds. *Sexual Underworlds of the Enlightenment.* Manchester: Manchester University Press, 1987.

Roussel, Roy. *The Conversation of the Sexes: Seduction and Equality in Selected Seventeenth- and Eighteenth-Century Texts.* New York: Oxford University Press, 1986.

Russo, Mary. "Female Grotesques: Carnival and Theory." In *Feminist Studies/Critical Studies.* Ed. Teresa de Lauretis, 213–29. Bloomington: Indiana University Press, 1986.

Schafer, Roy. "Narration in the Psychoanalytic Dialogue." In *On Narrative.* Ed. W. J. T. Mitchell, 25–49. Chicago: University of Chicago Press, 1981.

Schwartz, Lillian. "Leonardo's Mona Lisa." *Art and Antiques,* January 1987, 50–55.

Scott, Joan W. "Gender: A Useful Category of Historical Analysis." *The American Historical Review* 91 (December 1986): 1053–75.

Sedgwick, Eve Kosofsky. *Between Men: English Literature and Male Homosocial Desire*. New York: Columbia University Press, 1985.

Showalter, Elaine. "Critical Cross-Dressing: Male Feminists and the Woman of the Year." *Raritan* 3 (Fall 1983): 130–49.

Silverman, Kaja. "Fragments of a Fashionable Discourse." In *Studies in Entertainment: Critical Approaches to Mass Culture*. Ed. Tania Modleski, 139–52. Bloomington: Indiana University Press, 1986.

Smith, Sidonie. *A Poetics of Women's Autobiography: Marginality and the Fictions of Self-Representation*. Bloomington: Indiana University Press, 1987.

Spacks, Patricia Meyer. *The Female Imagination*. New York: Knopf, 1975.

——. *Imagining a Self: Autobiography and the Novel in Eighteenth-Century England*. Cambridge: Harvard University Press, 1976.

——. *John Gay*. New York: Twayne Publishers, 1965.

Spelman, Elizabeth V. "Woman as Body: Ancient and Contemporary Views." *Feminist Studies* 8 (Spring 1982): 109–32.

Spencer, Jane. *The Rise of the Woman Novelist: From Aphra Behn to Jane Austen*. New York: Basil Blackwell 1986.

Spender, Dale. *Mothers of the Novel: 100 Good Women Writers before Jane Austen*. New York: Pandora, 1986.

Stallybrass, Peter, and Allon White. *The Politics and Poetics of Transgression*. Ithaca: Cornell University Press, 1986.

Starr, George. *Defoe and Spiritual Autobiography*. Princeton: Princeton University Press, 1975.

Stoller, Robert J. *Observing the Erotic Imagination*. New Haven: Yale University Press, 1985.

——. *Presentations of Gender*. New Haven: Yale University Press, 1985.

——. *Sex and Gender*. Vol. I. *The Development of Masculinity and Femininity*. New York: Jason Aronson, 1968. Rpt. 1974.

Stone, Lawrence. *The Family, Sex, and Marriage in England, 1500–1800*. New York: Harper and Row, 1977.

Suleiman, Susan, ed. *The Female Body in Western Culture*. Cambridge: Harvard University Press, 1987.

Sutherland, James. *Defoe*. London: Methuen, 1937. Rpt. 1950.

Tanner, Tony. *Adultery in the Novel: Contract and Transgression*. Baltimore: Johns Hopkins University Press, 1979.

Taylor, Anne Robinson. *Male Novelists and Their Female Voices: Literary Masquerades*. Troy, N.Y.: Whitston Publishing, 1981.

Todd, Janet. *The Sign of Angellica: Women, Writing, and Fiction, 1660–1800*. New York: Columbia University Press, 1989.

Traugott, John. "*Clarissa*'s Richardson: An Essay to Find the Reader." In *English Literature in the Age of Disguise*. Ed. Maximillian E. Novak, 157–208. Berkeley: University of California Press, 1977.

Trumbach, Randolph. "London's Sodomites." *Journal of Social History* 11 (1977–78): 1–33.

——. "Modern Prostitution and Gender in *Fanny Hill*: Libertine and Domesticated Fantasy." In *Sexual Underworlds of the Enlightenment*. Ed. G. S. Rousseau and Roy Porter, Manchester: Manchester University Press, 1987.

Utter, Robert Palfrey, and Gwendolyn Bridges Needham. *Pamela's Daughters*. New York: Macmillan, 1937.

Van Ghent, Dorothy. *The English Novel: Form and Function*. New York: Rinehart, 1953.

Van Marter, Shirley. "Richardson's Revisions of *Clarissa* in the Second Edition." *Studies in Bibliography* 26 (1973): 107–32.

Ward, Ned. *The Secret History of the London Clubs*. 1709. London: 1956.

Warner, William B. *Reading Clarissa: The Struggles of Interpretation*. New Haven: Yale University Press, 1979.

Watt, Ian. *The Rise of the Novel: Studies in Defoe, Richardson, and Fielding*. Berkeley: University of California Press, 1957.

Western, J. R. *The English Militia in the Eighteenth Century*. London: Routledge and Kegan Paul, 1965.

Wiles, Roy M. "The Relish for Reading in Provincial England Two Centuries Ago." In *The Widening Circle: Essays on the Circulation of Literature in Eighteenth-Century Europe*. Ed. Paul J. Korshin, 87–115. Philadelphia: University of Pennsylvania Press, 1976.

Wilt, Judith. "He Could Go No Farther: A Modest Proposal about Lovelace and Clarissa." *PMLA* 92 (January 1977): 19–32.

Winkler, John J. *The Constraints of Desire: The Anthropology of Sex and Gender in Ancient Greece*. New York: Routledge, 1989.

Winnicott, D. W. *Through Paediatrics to Psycho-Analysis*. New York: Basic Books, 1958. Rpt. 1975.

Wise, Thomas N., and Jon K. Meyer. "Transvestism: Previous Findings and New Areas for Inquiry." *Journal of Sex and Marital Therapy* 6 (Summer 1980): 116–28.

Wollstonecraft, Mary. *Maria, or the Wrongs of Woman*. 1798. New York: W. W. Norton, 1975.

Woolf, Virginia. "Defoe." *The Common Reader*, 89–97. New York: Harcourt, Brace & World, 1935.

——. *Orlando*. New York: Harcourt, Brace & World, 1928.

——. "Robinson Crusoe." *The Second Common Reader*, 42–49. New York: Harcourt, Brace & World, 1960.

——. *A Room of One's Own*. New York: Harcourt, Brace & World, 1929.

Zeitlin, Froma I. "Travesties of Gender and Genre in Aristophanes' *Thesmophoriazousae*." *Critical Inquiry* 8 (Winter 1981): 301–28.

Index